Demand Side Economics:

A System that Works

I
Demand Side Minds

by

Alan Harvey

Publication data

Copyright © Alan Harvey 2012

Published in the United States by
Demand Side Books

ISBN-13: 978-1478205807
ISBN-10: 1478205806

First Edition
Published July 2012

e-books and
audio books available

DemandSideBooks.com

for Emily E.

mother to many, friend to all

Acknowledgements:

This has been the product of many years and much help. I would be remiss not to acknowledge in particular the assistance and encouragement and perspective of the indispensable Ranann Taylor and my old friend James Wright.

There are no doubt errors an omissions that remain, and these are the sole responsibility of the author.

DEMAND SIDE ECONOMICS

TABLE OF CONTENTS

Introduction

> *The belief that economic theory is sound, and
> that it alone considers 'the big picture', is the major
> reason why economics has gained such an ascendancy
> over public policy. Economists, we are told, know what
> is best for society because economic theory knows how a
> market economy works, and how it can be made to work
> better, to everyone's ultimate benefit. Its critics are
> simply special interest groups, at best misunder-
> standing the mechanisms of a market economy, at
> worst pleading their own special case to the detriment
> of the larger good. If we simply ignore the criticisms,
> and follow the guidelines of economic policy, ultimately
> everybody will be better off. The occasional failures of
> economies to respond as economic theory predicts occur
> because the relevant policy-makers either applied the
> theory badly, or were using out-of-date economics.*
> *Bunkum.*
> *If this proposition were true, then economic
> theory would be clear, unequivocal, unsullied, and
> empirically verified. It is nothing of the sort.*

Steve Keen

The purpose of this book is to lay out an economics that makes
sense of history, including the revolutionary history of the present time.
This "Demand Side" economics is not new. It was originated and developed
by the great British economist John Maynard Keynes and by the acolytes of
the pragmatic programs of the New Deal. It is called Demand Side eco-

nomics because demand is the fundamental driver of modern economies, and demand is the fundamental constraint in economic stagnation. The organization of demand is the organization of the economy. What is demanded is what is supplied, in scale and in selection. Employment, investment, growth and development occur along the path of what is demanded. That demand can be for public or private goods. We describe and display the Demand Side framework by following its development through the thought of a series of influential economists, beginning with Keynes and ending with Steve Keen and Nouriel Roubini. Through their work, concepts and analytical tools we can look in on the development of the modern economy since 1930.

The single largest obstacle for the reader may be to accept the notion that this relatively advanced line of economic thought has been marginalized by the mainstream orthodoxy over the past thirty years when it has proven to be valid and that orthodoxy has not. The orthodoxy as it is now practiced is as wrong as that which Ptolemaic astronomers used to view the universe, with the Earth at its center. The Demand Side Copernicans have been excommunicated from the church in policy, politics and academics. This is in spite of dozens of years of success through World War II and into the 1970s.

We will not burden our discussion with a systematic refutation of this orthodoxy, though references are littered throughout. But we establish the difference here, early, and in the strongest terms. To minimize the gulf would be to mischaracterize the intellectual geography. Adherents to the orthodoxy comprise the great majority of professional economists, but the same number failed to see the biggest economic event of the past 75 years. Those who did predict the financial crisis, and even the housing bubble that preceded it, were marginalized, and revealingly, are still excluded from the head tables of policy. This book is written in an era of change and economic turmoil for the purpose of clarifying basic economics and to bring to its readers a confidence of understanding. To the extent those readers rely on the orthodoxy, they will be disappointed.[1]

Steve Keen's conclusion is that *"economists have been educated into ignorance,"* or as he puts it more pungently:

---

[1] We acknowledge that the book is, ironically perhaps, and to a sad extent, the product of frustration. Personal frustration. Professional frustration. And frustration for the ineptitude of the discipline of economics over the past thirty years. We visit this personal frustration in the Afterword.

"Economics students therefore graduate from Masters and PhD programs with an effectively vacuous understanding of economics, no appreciation of the intellectual history of their discipline, and an approach to mathematics which hobbles both their critical understanding of economics, and their ability to appreciate the latest advances in mathematics and other sciences.

"A minority of these ill-informed students themselves go on to be academic economists, and then repeat the process. Ignorance is perpetuated.

"The attempt to conduct a critical dialogue within the profession of academic economics has therefore failed, not because economics has no flaws, but because — figuratively speaking — conventional economists have no ears."

(Keen, 2001)

We will suggest in this book that central bankers do not understand how money is created. Market-first economists imagine an economy that does not exist. General equilibrium forecasters propose an optimal equilibrium that does not exist. Elaborate mathematical expressions of the workings of the economy — "models" — present an elegant description, but of an entirely hypothetical world. Whole schools of economic thought, scores of careers, thousands of academic papers and texts are built on patently false assumptions. Models commonly used to predict, even in the aftermath of a financial crisis born in the banking system, do not include a banking sector. Massive private debt is ignored, while at the same time the public sector — government — is excoriated for somehow slipping back through time to be the cause of the financial crisis.

The corruption of the discipline has been fomented and abetted by the dominant corporate and political interests. One might think of the movie *Inside Job*, in which a few prominent economists were seen to have profited from slanting their opinion to the decided detriment of anyone who relied on their analysis. This problem is systemic, not isolated. Prominent academics sit on boards of financial corporations and take home enormous sums for the effort. Endowed seats at the most influential universities are filled with those who most accurately fulfill the purposes of the moneyed interests which endow them. These ties are rarely acknowledged, but common, and they fundamentally influence research and policy.

The selection of the most powerful institutional leaders and policy makers is made on the basis of corporate-friendly ideology, not competence. One thinks of Alan Greenspan — promoted by Ronald Reagan to direct the Federal Reserve, the nation's central bank — for nothing other than his Libertarian political bias. That anti-regulatory prejudice led to non-regulation and to sorry consequences for the world. But also think of his successor Ben Bernanke. Bernanke's academic reputation was as an expert on the Great Depression, and in particular his theory that the Depression could have been avoided by preventing the failure of banks. This bankers first hypothesis has been tested now by a massive intervention sponsored on behalf of the banks. The lives of these institutions have been extended. "Too big to fail" has grown ever larger. But economic misery for the rest has not been averted.

We have the spectacle of an establishment mainstream floundering intellectually in the presence of a stagnation they did not predict. Kenneth Rogoff, the acknowledged expert on financial crises, warning against an inflation that cannot come. Paul Krugman, an extremely liberal practitioner of the orthodoxy, bemoans a zero bound on interest rates that has no significance. In 2008 policy makers promised that recapitalizing banks and making corporations profitable was the road to recovery. Now that banks enjoy record capital reserves and corporations publish profits as never before, the recovery is redefined to look like stagnation. The promises are replaced by paternal assurances that *"these things take time."*

Jobs, physical and social infrastructure, and preparation for a looming climate crisis are all deemed too expensive to buy directly. This is exactly wrong. Direct spending on these critical needs is the route out of this Second Depression. Its template was set in the New Deal and ratified by the experiment of World War II. Substantial, disciplined, public demand righted the economy for all sectors — business, households, government — and for the future as well.

Through the 1960s and into the 1970s economics was a liberal discipline. As Juliet Schor has said, *"The discipline got more and more conservative over the 80s and 90s and into the 2000s. The reason for that is not anything rooted primarily in intellectual dynamics — but because economics is a highly political discipline that tends to move with the larger politics. As the politics in the country moved to the right, the discipline moved to the right."* (Schor, 2011)

The political conscience of the 1960s and 1970s influenced other academic disciplines — anthropology, history, sociology — in the opposite direction. Economics was captured in a concerted effort by financial and corporate elites. The Market was elevated to a level of omniscience, omnipotence and omnipresence. Unfortunately, market fundamentalism required of its adherents not only faith in its reliability, but fervor so complete as to obscure the empirical results. The manifest failures of the new, conservative, supply side economics included a lower growth rate, higher government deficits, stagnating median incomes, crumbling infrastructure, ever weaker social services, and increased vulnerability to financial ruin.

It is not the invisible hand of self-interest that has created the economic advances of mankind. It is only when the market is structured and the society is protected from Capitalism's inherent instability that the industry of the many is not confiscated by the few. It is only when the rule of law and the principles of fairness and equal opportunity are elevated that economic well-being is raised. It is only when the tools of industry — education being primary among them, but not alone — are available to the many, and the exercise of these tools is not restricted except by an individual's capacity, that the full flower of an economy is possible.

By these lights, the deregulation of finances and of the marketplace is absurd and destructive, as it allows the domination by the powerful and entrenched and ruthless. It allows the game to be refereed by the strongest players. The reduction of shared tools of industry, by the deterioration of public goods and the Commons, is likewise corrosive to well-being. Legal structures that enforce fairness and equal treatment, as well as roads, education, police and the rest, are shared by all. They are not limited in their utility to one or to a small group. These are the water and the soil of an economy, without which the individual seeds cannot flower or bear fruit. When these goods are restricted by entrenched interest or ignorance or avarice, the fields are depleted and the harvest is reduced for all.

The contention that moral or spiritual principles apply everywhere but in the realm of finance, business and economics — where greed must have its day — is a contention born of self-interest, not objective science.

As we discover here, cooperation and support to the "least of these" has economic dynamics as compelling as competition and favoritism to the powerful. There is absolutely no need to cede the economic argument. In spite of its impressive sponsorship, the economics of the powerful continues to fail. And contrary to conservative orthodoxy, there are no economic tides which ebb and flow according to natural economic forces and immutable rhythms obscure from human understanding. There are only the interests of the world and its people. Incentives and financial architecture can be designed to fit the purposes of the society. Markets can be structured and do not need to be abandoned to the control of the dominant market players. The society need not contort to fit the economics. The economics can be designed for the benefit of the society. Indeed, the invisible hand is blind, so it must be guided. Structure and guidance is much more efficient than enabling a free market road to nowhere.

A last note: This is not a book for economists. Some may see it as a book AGAINST economists. It is instead a book for people concerned with public policy. Whether or not the reader accepts all the arguments and observations here, we hope he or she will admit that the scope and perspective is appropriate and the stakes are accurately calibrated. The minutia and sophistry usual to economics is a realm of distraction we can no longer afford. We need a lens to penetrate the confusion of competing theories and explanations. That lens exists, in a sophisticated form. It has been applied in previous, equally difficult times to great effect.

Chapter 1:

Many Parts

> *The ideas of economists and political philosophers,*
> *both when they are right and when they are wrong, are more*
> *powerful than is commonly understood. Indeed the world is*
> *ruled by little else. Practical men, who believe themselves to be*
> *quite exempt from any intellectual influence, are usually the*
> *slaves of some defunct economist.*

John Maynard Keynes

This is a book of **history**, a book *of statistics*, a book of **theory**, but at its base it is a book of a few big words.

This is a book of history because economics takes its meaning from its historical context. Economic and financial institutions are born, developed, reformed, manipulated, and in time they age and die. The growth of industries, the relationship of classes, the development of the state — all are economic processes and events. In this evolution it becomes obvious that economics and politics are entwined. The public purpose is the purpose of enlightened economics. The economic challenges are not abstract. They are the issues of the day. Economic tools have been developed to meet the real world, and they can be startlingly useful. Sad to say, however, that many more tools have been developed at great cost and employed with great fanfare to meet hypothetical worlds. The result here is inevitable confusion and distortion. The economics profession is recognized primarily in the form of men of august diplomas who have risen in one or another order of a priesthood most political and insular. The economics of today is not the economics of fifty years ago nor fifty years hence, but the discussion is conducted as if it is.

This is a book of statistics and case studies because economics ought to be the most practical discipline. Its concerns should be with what works and how to get to there from here. While statistics are often designed to prove the statistician's intent ("designer statistics"), they can be evidence and proof if used correctly and transparently.

And this is a book of theory simply because theory is the brain behind economic vision. Why does it work? How does the mind of the aggregate reflect the mind of the individual? How can the whole be made safe and free and fair for its member parts? Why does the greatest good arise in democratic society?

But at its base it is a book of a few big words. Some of the words may be familiar. Some may not be recognizable. *Demand Side. Supply Side. Free-Market Capitalism. Corporate Oligarchy. Conservative, Classical, or Neoclassical Economics. The Commons. Public Goods.*

Demand Side may be the least trafficked word. Most will initially understand it as a counter to *Supply Side,* the economic fad of the Reagan era that failed so well then, again under George W. Bush, and continues to fail wherever it is tried. But Demand Side's history is longer and more noble. It was not developed as a rationale for political manipulation, but from an analysis of events. It began in the 1930s. One of its two major streams organized around the academic work of the great British economist John Maynard Keynes. The second stream arose from the New Deal and its army of motivated public servants who produced the pragmatic combination of social insurance, market regulation and government direction of the economy. The theory and practice of Demand Side were borne out by the Great Depression and the Second World War, as well as by the prosperity and political stability that followed the War. Demand Side, or a flavor of it, organized economic thought into the 1970s.

The Demand Side description here follows this combined stream of Keynesian and New Deal thinking through the work of nine great economists, some known, some not so well known: John Maynard Keynes, Leon Keyserling, John Kenneth Galbraith, Hyman Minsky, Joseph Stiglitz, James K. Galbraith, George Soros, Steve Keen and Nouriel Roubini.

Supply Side was a short-lived, ideologically-driven experiment in Pollyanna-ism which proved a failure as an economic school, but lucrative to the political backers of then president Ronald Reagan. Contrast this with Demand Side, which is not a belief system, but a science of economics that has been developed, examined and proven, and continues to prove out. Supply Side's tenets held that, if freed from government red tape and restrictions on the scale of reward, the market would unleash new waves of growth and prosperity. These promises quickly faded in recession and debt. This was economics, as Thorsten Veblen put it, as "*an exercise in ceremonial adequacy.*" Supply Side is a big word with a small meaning. It was promulgated by the powerful and most often accorded only with the interests of power. It is only by the power of its sponsors that it remains alive today in quasi-independent institutions such as the Heritage Foundation and American Enterprise Institute, and in universities with close connections to the financial and corporate sectors.

      Free-Market Capitalism is a big word indeed. It represents the concept that a vibrant provisioning of the planet's people is possible only by conceding the incentives and the primary virtue to the pursuit of profit. The free market's titular prophet was Adam Smith. His "invisible hand" is as close as many economists get to theology. The invisible hand proposes that optimal amounts of production will be induced not by command or compulsion, but by the great virtue of personal interest responding to the signals of the market. While Smith laid much less emphasis on the invisible hand than do his modern promoters, he is now the icon for the idea that, if left unfettered by governmental interference, the Market can identify what is needed, where, how much, and can discipline the producers who disobey. This is, John Kenneth Galbraith wrote in his **Economics in Perspective**, "*a celebration of approved belief ... thought founded not on what is actual but on what is agreeable and convenient to the influential interest.*" (Galbraith J. K., 1987)

      As we look at the work of the elder Galbraith, we will see that the market is not free, but controlled and controlled most often by the corporate giants whose existence is assumed away by Free Marketeers. Nor does the optimal complement of goods come into existence, magically or otherwise, but most often only those goods which produce wealth for the wealthy. The product of pollution, global warming, mind-numbing jobs, poverty and ignorance are, in economist-speak "externalities" to this free market, but are *external* only to the sacred event of purchase and sale. But the farce is more tragic than this. "Free market" has been strapped to an idea of liberty, so that in the popular mind, the society is "free" from government domination. This is freedom only in the Orwellian sense of being yoked to the interests of a dominant elite. **Free market economics** is a word as big as Oz, describing a power that purports to see everywhere, but in reality is limited to a small screen and limited stage.

      Corporate Oligarchy. When this term is defined, it will be instantly recognized as the fact of current economic structure in the United States. An *oligopoly* is an economic term referring to the control of a market by a few large firms, the reality of the market as opposed to the free-market fantasy. *Oligarchy* is the control of the state by a few people. *Corporate Oligarchy* refers to control of the state and the economy by corporate interests: Big Pharma, Auto, Defense, Big Oil, Wall Street. The defining contest of the present day is the competition between representative democracy and this Corporate Oligarchy for control of the state.

Neoclassical Economics is a primarily academic pursuit which posits stability and optimal outcomes in terms of employment and use of capacity as a natural to a market economy. Invisible hand economics is assumed to lead to the best for all. More than this, the economy attains the status of being a viable organism, not simply an organizational scheme or composite of competing interests. Neoclassical economics takes the whole to be a system with internal integrity, a machine whose workings are naturally self-balancing, "in equilibrium." With this assumption, mathematical analysis can be applied as if to a physical thermodynamic system. "Optimal equilibrium" outcomes are notably absent from Demand Side expectations. In some ways it is congruent with free-market capitalism. It is to free market capitalism as the Bible is to a religious tract, more complete, but less simplistic, and infinitely more susceptible to interpretation.

Classical economics took quite a blow from reality with the advent of the Great Depression of the 1930s. It then made a strong comeback by incorporating some superficial aspects of Keynesianism and rebranding itself as "Neoclassical" (or even "New Keynesian"). By rights, after the Great Financial Crisis of 2008, it should again be in deep defensive mode. Always behind the curve, its purpose seems not so much to assist the survival of the world's civilizations as to provide (in paraphrase of Galbraith the elder) non-offensive employment to professors and instructors. And it is by this control of academia, the leading economics association (the American Economics Association), the most prestigious journals, the textbooks that frame the subject of economics, and the basic narrative that Neoclassical economics retains its hold on the formal discipline of economics. The result, sadly, is a busload of emperors with no clothes, since the rest of literate society recognizes its shortcomings. Its tenuous hold on respectability often depends on abstruse mathematical applications. Not only is economic mathematics a special and somewhat dated version of mathematics, but the typical mathematical exercise relates to historical reality in the same way the reaction in a Petri dish relates to evolution. There is a certain similarity in pattern, but the scale and gravity is of a different dimension. Unrealistic, simplistic, myopic assumptions remove findings from the world of relevance to the laboratory of peripheral interest.

The Commons is an elementary economics word which originally referred to pasture held in common by villagers. Today the Commons is rightly seen as the air, the water, ecosystems and resources shared or used in common. The *Tragedy of the Commons* is the full title for the original observation. *Tragedy* because inevitably the Commons, without restrictions to use, became overgrazed and barren, for there was no incentive for any one user to show responsibility. If his cow was restrained from the pasture, another's would take its place. So also in addition to barren pasture, the Commons produced gaunt and profitless cattle. Overuse of the world's ecosystems and resources by the same incentives and absence of restrictions are producing those dreadful outcomes on a planetary scale. New institutions, foresight and the moral fortitude to take responsibility for the Commons is the necessary next step in evolution.

Public Goods are in distinction to **private goods**. The market produces private goods, individually consumed goods, from candy bars to cars, in abundance. Public goods are not produced so abundantly. Because of the inherent characteristics of not being excludable or depletable (and notably not for any absence of value), public goods are the province of federal, state and local governments. These essential goods and services include roads, police, education, national defense, courts and prisons, some health and social services, libraries, and so on. **Public goods** is a big word because it is by way of public goods that prosperity is seeded, nurtured, grown and ripened. Public goods have been the platform upon which every prosperous society has risen. We will argue that policy which prefers that private goods dominate is a route not to well-being, but demonstrably, to instability and failure.

In large part the critical path is blocked by the entrenched corporate control of the economy and abetted by an economics of confusion. This confusion is an artifact of the opposition of powerful institutions, not any academic or intellectual virtue. Those issues, obstacles, challenges and threats which society must solve for its own survival and which will need the organization of economics are purposely muddled by insiders and their political power brokers. Global climate change, desperate poverty in the Third World, immigration, loss of democratic control of political institutions, inability to adapt, all are connected in an economic context and through economic institutions that have been radically compromised for private profit.

But we offer a way forward. It may be surprising, given the harsh terms employed in the description of the problem, that the remedies here are seemingly so mild. Certainly "mild" is not the word which is employed by the affected special interests, but mild they are. One eye has been kept on political practicality, to be sure, because a remedy is no remedy if it cannot be applied. For example, the cleansing of market pricing from manipulation by corporations ought to be amenable to theoretical conservatives as well as progressives. It is those who employ the tenets of a free market faith in their sermons, but whose purpose is not to support such economics, rather to excuse corporate control, who will be most exercised. The tax code can be dedicated to its primary purpose of providing revenue to the government in a non-distortionary way. Ulterior purposes, such as subsidizing one or another industry or activity are not strictly appropriate. Subsidies, at least in theory, could be provided above board with direct payments.

This proposal is imminently do-able and probably least dubious in theory, but is no doubt extremely difficult politically. Elsewhere, the value of public goods is not so much controversial as it is misunderstood. A fair look at public goods and the necessity of maintaining the Commons would lead to approval in most eyes.

We also draw attention here to a proposition not widely agreed to, but essential to the Demand Side. That is that the well-being of the poor and middle class are of infinitely more importance than that of the wealthy, not only because there are more of them, but because when they do better the whole does better. The great nonsense of modern times is that wealthy individuals and countries are so by necessity, to keep some sort of economic machinery running smoothly, or that it makes little difference to an abstraction of economic efficiency how few or how many collect the bulk of income or exercise the bulk of spending. Quite the opposite is the case. When well-being is concentrated in a few, imbalances are created that not only produce immoral poverty and deprivation, but that threaten a successful progress into the future. Personal security cannot be the province only of the wealthy, nor can the incentives to do better be confined to the upper percentiles.

Demand Side's superiority in this contest is demonstrable. Comparing historical eras within the U.S., when the society has invested in public goods, all segments have done better in terms of income growth. Likewise, comparing outcomes across nations, those economies with higher investment in public goods have done better. Income equality is found in societies with better personal and social health outcomes, and *vice versa*, better outcomes attend societies with more equal incomes.

Chapter 2:

Three Challenges
and the Demand Side Approach

> *Economics and particularly the imagery of choice in the market puts the business firm in the service of a higher deity. It is not responsible for what it does. It responds to the theistic instruction of the market. If the goods that it produces or the services that it renders are frivolous or lethal or do damage to air, water, landscape or the tranquility of life, the firm is not to blame. This reflects the public choice. If people are abused, it is because they choose self-abuse. If economic behavior seems on occasion insane, it is because people are insane.*

John Kenneth Galbraith

Everything is possible in Wonderland. It is a place where market choices and personal self-interest produce ever more consumer goods for an ever-growing world population. If clouds should appear, say climate change, production and consumption will by internal magic become environmentally benign. There is nothing to do. Just trust in the market. If we step out of Wonderland into a real world, a world rife with hunger, with accelerating environmental change, where wealth is dissolving into an ocean of debt illuminated by the flashing lights of casino capitalism, there is much to do.

Nothing can save us when materialism is assumed to be genetic and venality the primary human trait. If the individual will always subvert the community to his own small purpose, then the community cannot protect the individual or her descendents. Economics is, or ought to be, the discipline of social organization. Successful economics is a science that explains successful social organization in terms of survival and prosperity. Further, as we will illustrate, democracy, equality and justice are not ***normative***, that is, values which follow from ethical codes outside economics, but are ***positive***, principles which organize and energize prosperous and coherent development. Substantial institutions of property rights and contract law, for example, are ground upon which a healthy economy grows. No less so are other institutions of civil organization and empowerment, and ultimately institutions of public property rights and community protection. There is a symmetry of democratic values and economic efficiency that is observable and at least statistically provable. But unless we test our principles, they remain hypotheses. While there are no laboratory experiments for economics, there is the experience of history. History is the laboratory of economics.

No more absurd expression of the hubris of orthodox economics is its insistence on prescriptions long after those prescriptions have sickened or even killed the patient. In this book we test principles in a reading of history and human experience, particularly related to three major challenges: The challenge of the environmental collapse of the planet, the challenge of global poverty, and the challenge of the economic decline of the United States. The debate in this contest will be from claimants made for the consumer society, for corporate control, for materialism, as well as for those from the various orthodox and classical schools. Setting the context for that debate, we outline the challenges a little further.

The Environment

The deterioration of global ecosystems has been chronicled in a drumbeat of scientific reports. No longer is it possible for any but the intentionally myopic to avoid seeing the need for concerted action. There will be no escape or substitute for addressing the causes and reversing the symptoms of global warming. Rising sea levels, the deforestation of vast tracts, receding glaciers, stalling sea currents, disappearing phytoplankton, the pitiless march of desertification, the demise of any one of a dozen natural systems could send the Earth spinning off its climatic axis.

Wider appreciation of the impending calamities is avoided only by fearful denial or purposeful ignorance. The hesitance of many scientists to be more aggressive in advocacy has not helped, nor has a cynical campaign of disinformation waged on behalf of industrial interests who poison the environmental future, but who are content to thrive in the current market. Public policy which enables the current *laissez faire* scheme or delays aggressive action is, in fact, denial of the true dimensions of the crisis unfolding.

It has been argued specifically that the United States can do nothing about these problems because of the economics. Adaptation and remediation will, it is claimed, be a burden to its consumers and its industrial base. We cannot afford it, so our plan must be an abject hope, hope that markets will produce what the future demands rather than track the desires of today's consumers and industrialists. Demand Side sees the solution in a direction 180 degrees from this. No industrial advance — from interchangeable parts to the Internet — has been possible without public demand. We can choose how to employ our resources, labor and capital. It is a choice we now make by default, or by a corrupt process of competing constituencies, with the representative bodies acting as marketplaces themselves, and policies following the auction to the highest bidder. Economic life is a matter of human design. Its institutions, incentives and relationships are consciously arranged. Any parallel between this arrangement of human institutions and the natural balances that are now threatened is drawn in error.

Environmentally conservative and productive industries are economically of equal or greater value than those which destroy. (We will see later how the accounting has been rigged in favor of current consumption.) The development of new energy systems and transportation technologies have driven vigorous economies in the past. They could do so again. The established interests, threatened by adaptation to future needs, employ a tactic which entrenched interests have used for centuries — the proposition that society cannot afford the change. In this case, it is the absurd proposition that a society cannot afford its own survival.

More specifically, when scientists say climate change is caused by "human activity," the human activity is the burning of fossil fuels in an amount that creates greenhouse gases — the energy generation for industry, the heating and cooling of buildings and the animation of hundreds of millions of motor vehicles. This human activity can be altered in the short term using the capacity now idled. In the medium term, new energy sources and techniques to conserve energy use must be developed. Long-term survival will require a new development path for nations. We cannot afford what we already see in India, China and others — a desperate rush to development utilizing the same dirty energy technology that has pushed the planet to the brink. China, the new industrial giant, for example, may become the world's first failed state environmentally even as it dominates economically. (Economy, 2004)

A Demand Side economics can order costs and prices in a rational way and generate a truly productive economy. The market mechanism can be freed from control not by the bogeyman of an interfering government, but by the actual manipulation of dominating corporations.

World Poverty

Free market capitalism applies only to the world's people who can participate in markets — those with money. Fully three billion inhabitants of our planet, half its population, subsist on less than $2 per day. (Ramonet, 1998) The World Bank identifies 1.3 billion people living on less than $1 per day. A billion people cannot read or write at even the most rudimentary levels. (UNICEF, 1999)

The United Nations *Millennium Development Goals* define a program of rescue, not development. Global health problems, which comprise several of the goals, are more properly problems of poverty, malnutrition and want.[1]

At the same time, we engage in a national and regional policy of governmental competition with our trading partners. "Competing" with our "partners" does not raise an eyebrow. The competition is to produce the most for least. When it infects public policy it means that huge costs are shuffled out of the market and onto the public purse. These are the so-called "externalities" — environmental degradation and human deprivation among them. The Commons is exploited for private gain, and necessary public goods go wanting.

Nations should cooperate for the common good. The corporations in the supposed free market are those who should compete. Instead, as Joseph Stiglitz points out, the world's most powerful nation seeks to dominate the weaker and often for the benefit of major corporate interests. By way of the World Bank and International Monetary Fund (IMF) radical market fundamentalist economic schemes and suffocating national budget requirements are prescribed for developing economies. These are strictures we in the U.S., even as conservative as we have become, would never approach in practice. They were never seriously considered when economic crisis visited our shores. As we will see, instead of factories and exportable commodities and debt, these undeveloped nations could be building roads, schools, infrastructure, utilities and reinforcing their basic agrarian economies. They could be building a future not dependent on Western consumerism, but collaborative in a broad prosperity. "Globalization" too often means plantationism, more miserable than serfdom because workers do not have the rights even of soil.

While it is possible for a minority of nations to develop on an export model, it is not possible for all. To be successful — as with China, Japan and South Korea — it requires net exporters to send capital as well. The fact of developing

---

[1] Immigration, an issue which has aroused such fear in the United States, is a function of impoverishment of Mexico and other Latin American countries. This is an economic and trade problem, not an issue of border security.

nations financing the consumption of developed nations is only slightly less absurd than the acceptance of free market capitalism as a success on a planet burdened with such savage poverty.

The Economic Decline of the United States

It is a mistake in fundamental understanding to believe the economic troubles of the U.S. began with the financial crisis of 2008. While this may be the understanding upon which public policy is made, along with the implicit corollary that return to normal is just around the corner, it is far from true. The Great Financial Crisis stemmed from financial markets left to design themselves and a resulting housing bubble whose collapse has destroyed trillions of dollars of wealth while leaving the debt incurred to finance it standing on the balance sheets of tens of millions of households. It needs to be emphasized, however, that this bubble did not help the real economy. The entire exercise of the first decade of the 2000s produced not one single net new job.

Now an aging population enters retirement with its Social Security made fragile by decades of borrowing from its trust funds to float general government operations, tax cuts and foreign wars. Health care now demands one-sixth of economic output — twice the proportion of other industrial nations — while providing a lower level of service as measured by health outcomes. The nation is in the advanced stages of losing its manufacturing base. The broader industrial base, which includes its transportation, energy and utility infrastructure, is crumbling. Its social capital, the health and skills and education of its population, has declined along a similarly steep slope.

What has grown over the past thirty years is the disparity between rich and poor, the proportion of the economy's profit that goes to the financial sector, and the power of that financial sector over the political institutions. What has also grown is debt and borrowing, and not primarily the well-publicized government debt. Government debt has expanded from 50 percent of GDP in 2000 to over 80 percent in 2011. Over the same period private debt grew from 200 percent of GDP in 2000 to over 300 percent in 2009, before falling back sharply to around 260 percent.

It is important to realize that this debt is money spent. The borrowings of the 2000s, 1990s and 1980s have been spent. Economic activity financed by that borrowing masked the fundamental deterioration of the economy and stagnation of incomes. At this point, paying down the debt by households and balancing budgets by government may improve balance sheets, but to see this as a way to return to vigorous economic activity is an illusion.

But while the collapse is evident, the addiction to consumption patterns of the past continues, and even more ruinously, to the failed economic policies, explanations and relationships.

Demand Side Solutions

It is absolutely critical to employ Demand Side concepts in place of the failed free market nostrums. These concepts are not startling new ideas to economics, although to many of the economists of the past generation they may seem revolutionary. They are part and parcel of what has worked.

Output is determined by effective demand. Demand is the sum of incomes and net borrowing. It was inflated by the debt boom and will be contracted by debt repayments. But all demand is not equal. Spending which generates employment has follow-on benefits, as new job-holders demand additional goods and services. This is a process known as the *multiplier*. This multiplier works best with public investment (public works), less well with tax cuts for consumers, and not at all with benefits provided directly to producers. At the same time, public goods have real economic and financial benefits that commonly surpass those of private goods, often by factors of two, three, four, or more. So emphasizing these activities which lead to higher demand can at the same time improve the industrial base and social capital.

But adding another layer of economic policy will do little good alone. *It is also necessary to cleanse the market of its Supply Side bias.* This does not mean excessive regulation of the market participants, but does mean a structuring of the markets and an insistence that the market transaction include all costs, including those of so-called *externalities*, and at the same time not advantage the seller in information, nor the private sector by subsidizing demand manipulation.

Monetary policy must operate from an understanding of how money works, how it is created in the credit system, and how government can use its power over fiat money effectively. "Commodity money" is that which derives its value for the most part from the substance out of which it is made — gold, silver, copper. "Fiat money" derives its value from the government which issues it. "Credit money" is created in the financial system, which has a multitude of ways of creating credit money, the simplest of which is the fractional banking system, in which a dollar of deposits is often justification for ten dollars worth of loans. Since all effective demand is monetary, a government which understands how money is created and used has a powerful tool. Unfortunately, this is not the case at present, when the official producer of fiat money, the central bank (Federal Reserve in the U.S.) misses its mark every time. In particular, the Fed's policies promote ever more debt and advantage casino capitalism, financial investments, at the expense of real investment and real economic development.

The market needs to be transparent and understandable. The exchange between buyer and seller is the only opportunity for accountability in the private market. That is, the products being sold need to be well-defined and homogenous. The buyers' disadvantage with regard to information about products needs to be offset by a public oversight function that ensures safety and freedom from fraud. Costs not included in the purchase price and shunted aside under the rubric "externalities" for other, unnamed actors to deal with, are effectively the proof of market inefficiency. Markets can be well described in terms of products and warrantees.

It is necessary to take producers of consumer goods off steroids by eliminating the subsidy to demand manipulation. Advertising, promotion, bribery, lobbying and all such activities that are not directly connected to producing the good or service need to be dramatically restricted. Certainly they need not be subsidized by deductibility from taxation. This, again, does not mean new regulation, simply an end to tax deductions that are back door subsidies.

The developing world must be given an alternative path to development by way of investment in their infrastructure and social capital — not in plantations, resource extraction, or labor exploitation. A necessary first step is the removal of the unfair and crippling burden of debt. A second step, also necessary, is protection in trade agreements for their agrarian economies.

Most difficult of all is the essential requirement to reform the governance of the world's people to remove the dominance of the corporate oligarchy. It is essential to recognize this true structure of our economy and society. It is the rule by and needs of the corporate oligarchy that are the major obstacles to survival. To expect corporations to become docile or go away and submit their dominant positions meekly is, of course, unrealistic. Politically they are the most powerful at every level — local, state, national and international. On the other hand, according to polling, most Americans believe corporations have inordinate power. In a truly democratic contest they would be defeated. Simultaneously, it is not possible for corporations to continue to profit after the society in which they exist crumbles.

Where short-term corporate and long-term public interest are directly in opposition, the way forward will be confrontational, but a development path determined by whichever market force dominates is no longer affordable. Reducing that confrontation, in the context of the realities of the new millennium, however, is the possibility that the dominant companies can be invited and enabled to reinvent themselves. New energy sources, reformed transportation systems, low-chemical models for food production, and so on, are public goods which the corporate oligarchy has eschewed because they cannot themselves maintain and control these markets. In some cases, government should guarantee markets — i.e., price and quantity — so corporations can shift from exploitation of their current power to a targeted industrial development and a partnership with the public sector. In other cases, for public goods, it is the government itself which will be the buyer. The government contract is a clear, reliable description of cash flow that can be expected by a corporation. As Minsky points out, this sturdy return is exactly and all that is needed to lever private investment in capital, and it is no longer in prospect for the consumer economy.

Corporations are adept at handling complex technological, industrial and organizational tasks. The long-term interests of their owners is broadly aligned with the long-term interests of the society at large. However, as John Kenneth Galbraith pointed out long ago, owners (shareholders) do not control the corporations. These owners' interests are in practice subservient to the more short-term interests of directors and managers. But to the extent that all recognize that the returns to real investment in public goods are substantial and secure, those whose concern is the real economy will help remove those whose venue is the casino.

This is a practical way forward, completely in line with substantial and stable profits. It is a fundamental change from the consumer economy. In a public goods recovery, there is no less consumption. In fact, there is more. It is the nature of the goods that changes. Rather than private goods (consumer goods of all types, from baubles to food and clothing to housing and cars), it is public goods which are emphasized (education, public health, infrastructure, climate stability, public security, and so on).

It is a cruel myth that economic activity is orchestrated by natural laws and revolves in a manner to which governmental policy always amounts to interference, a reduction in efficiency, a distortion. Economic affairs have evolved to favor the powerful in every society. When the people are powerful, as in a free democracy, they are favored and the economy does well. When not, financial rewards cant to the dominant institution or group and economies sputter or stall.

It is, then, not populations that must bow to the natural laws of an economic galaxy. Instead the institutions, rules and incentives of the economic galaxy must be ordered to benefit populations.

Chapter 3:

Demand Side Minds: An Overview

> *Economics is the religion of the present.*
>
> **- Thorsten Veblen**

Demand Side economics arose from the work of John Maynard Keynes, but also from the pragmatic recovery work of the Roosevelt New Deal. Keynesianism and the New Deal conspired to mold policies that became the practical economic blueprint for the United States from the 1930s into the 1970s. This period includes the Great Depression and its tentative recoveries, the mobilization for war and the execution of that war (an effort which is Demand Side's most unheralded success), the difficult and highly successful transition from war to peace across the Western World, and the building of a prosperous new economy while at the same time managing the tremendous national debt that was the legacy of the war. The post-war prosperity, stability and employment were unprecedented in human history. They were direct results of Demand Side's policies.

In the following chapters we look at this history and that of subsequent years by means of capsule treatments of some of the best practitioners of the discipline: **John Maynard Keynes**, New Deal insider and later Truman's chief economist **Leon Keyserling**, the great writer and intellect **John Kenneth Galbraith**, maverick financial Keynesian **Hyman Minsky**, the ruthlessly insightful **Joseph Stiglitz**, the stubbornly idealistic and liberal, intellectual heir to his father, **James K. Galbraith**, philanthropist and market pathologist **George Soros**, mathematician and forecaster **Steve Keen**, and the eclectic forecaster and crisis analyst **Nouriel Roubini**. In this chapter, we present a preview of each.

John Maynard Keynes and the Great Depression

It is often and correctly said that John Maynard Keynes rescued capitalism from itself. He rejected the economics he found, and his thought was the originating point for the discipline of macroeconomics. Seventy years after he began, forty years after he had apparently triumphed, Keynes was reduced to a footnote in Economics 101. Five years after that he once again became the dominant mind of modern market capitalism, and the lessons he taught were being learned, painfully, again.

The Great Depression was a fundamental contradiction to the free market capitalism of the time. An identical contradiction confronts virtually the same ideology today. The causes of the Depression have been extensively debated, but whatever the cause, it was the failure to cure that led to the rejection of the orthodoxy. Lingering and worsening conditions, year after year — stagnation, decline, unemployment, deflation — sternly contradicted those who promised *"Recovery is just around the corner."* In Neoclassical equilibrium theory, such conditions could not persist for any meaningful length of time. When they did persist, then as now, politics demanded learning and adaptation. When the response from Wall Street and Academia was denial, their orthodoxy was rejected. Keynes and the New Deal under Roosevelt moved a new economics into the arena of government and public policy.

Keynes identified a paucity of effective demand as the cause of economic downturns. It is the strength and direction and composition of demand which organizes and energizes a society's economy. (This means effective demand, of course, not simply an intense desire, or even a desperate need, but a demand with real money behind it.)

Keynes argued that economic activity did not return to adequate levels because there was nothing to draw it there. If people do not earn an income because there is nobody to buy their goods or services, there immediately arises a demand problem that is self-reinforcing. Further, Keynes said, the appropriate remedy for lagging incomes and demand from consumers is government-sponsored demand via deficit spending — spending financed not by tax revenue, but by borrowing.

Keynes famously wrote:

> **"If the Treasury were to fill old bottles with bank-notes, bury them at suitable depths in disused coalmines which are then filled up to the surface with town rubbish, and leave it to private enterprise on well-tried principles of**

laissez-faire to dig the notes up again (the right to do so being obtained, of course, by tendering for leases of the note-bearing territory), there need be no more unemployment and, with the help of the repercussions, the real income of the community, and its capital wealth also, would probably become a good deal greater than it actually is. It would, indeed, be more sensible to build houses and the like; but if there are political and practical difficulties in the way of this, the above would be better than nothing."

(Keynes, 1936, p. 129)

The stabilization of the economy under the New Deal ratified its tenets. World War II and its economic organization ratified Keynesianism. This was a public works program on sufficient scale. It recalled Keynes' bottles and ten pound notes. War was made of products and services that were entirely destructive or would eventually be destroyed. In spite of this, the economy also produced more consumer goods for the people on the home front.

The sophisticated economic organization and mobilization for war on the Allied side was made possible by Keynes' concepts. The statistical profile of this new definition of the economy was pioneered and developed by Simon Kuznets in the form of the National Income and Product Accounts. The NIPA accounting framework is still the way we describe the economy to each other half a century later. (It should be noted here that, while Kuznets' work was a major accomplishment in economics and is enormously useful to this day, it does not properly display resource depletion, the consumption of the Commons, and other aspects of the real economy that are essential to the society's well-being going forward.)

Keynes himself was in the center of war planning for Britain and was a guiding force behind the Bretton Woods Conference of 1944, which organized the world's currency regime and financial relationships for the postwar economy. He died in 1946 at the age of 61. At that time he was the most famous economist in the world, and his reputation only grew in the decades after.

Leon Keyserling, the New Deal and the Postwar Prosperity

Demand Side economics arose during the Great Depression and was ratified by the experience of World War II. The first major impulse for its birth was the revolutionary thought of Keynes. The second was the pragmatic work to mitigate the suffering of the population by New Deal Democrats. Deficit spending recommended itself to activist economists in Franklin Roosevelt's New Deal, but not so much as a means of creating effective demand as much as a way of miti-gating the suffering of the unemployed, aged, disabled and impoverished. Financing these programs in the absence of an ability by the government to raise sufficient revenue created the deficit spending Keynes prescribed.

> **"The bulk of economists never have realized that the whole problem, the whole American economic problem, is ultimately the improved distribution of income. If we solve that, we solve all of the problems. That's all the inflationary problem really is, because it doesn't matter if prices are going up through programs which improve the distribution. If we had had the price inflation [written in May, 1971] that we have had in the last few years through policies which created full employment and did justice to the old people, and cleared slums and renewed our cities and cleared up polluted air and water, the same amount of inflation pur-chased at that cost would be the best bargain you could ever drive."**
>
> (Keyserling, 1971)

Leon Keyserling is, of the economists featured here, no doubt the least well-known today. He came to Washington in the early 1930s along with the best minds of a generation drawn to the greatest challenge of the generation. Keyserling found a role in New Deal policy from the outset, being the chief drafts-man of the **Wagner Act** in 1935, the single most important piece of labor legislation of the Twentieth Century . Keyserling also structured the signal piece of economics legislation in American History, the **Full Employment Act of 1946**. He managed economic policy under Harry Truman, conducting a successful transition from war to peace and setting in place the pillars for postwar prosperity. And late in life he materially assisted in the **Full Employment Act**'s sequel, the **Humphrey-Hawkins Bill**.

Keyserling was no doubt the most powerful of all chairs of the President's Council of Economic Advisers. But — in a comment more telling about its authors than its subject — many mainstream and academic economists have discounted Keyserling for his never having completed his PhD. Keyserling is not just a place holder for the genius of the New Deal. He was a powerful exponent of an eco-nomics that worked. It must be understood that after the War the United States was favored in industrial competition with the rest of the world by virtue of the destruction of the competing industry of Europe and Japan, but the broad pros-perity that visited the U.S. in the 1950s and 1960s was made possible by the "partnership" economics forged by the fiery Keyserling. His understanding also keyed the engagement of the U.S. internationally, as displayed in the Marshall Plan for the rebuilding of Europe, the Cold War support of nations across the world and the policy of containment of the Soviet Union.

John Kenneth Galbraith and the Rise of the Corporate State

As were Keynes and Keyserling, American economist John Kenneth Galbraith was integral to executing economic policy as a public servant at the highest levels. Like Keynes, Galbraith was an influential writer. Canadian born, schooled at Harvard and Berkeley, Galbraith moved into the federal government at the outset of World War II. He directed the Office of Price Administration, the second most powerful civilian post in the management of the wartime economy. Galbraith was literally controller of prices in the United States, charged with keeping wartime shortages from turning into crippling inflation or spawning corrosive black markets. At the War's conclusion, Galbraith directed the post-mortem survey and analysis of the German war industry and economy. His group reported out a surprising ineptness of the German economic organization (and at the same time cast doubt on the effectiveness of Allied bombing). (Summary Report, United States Strategic Bombing Survey, 1945) Under John F. Kennedy, Galbraith served as ambassador to India.

Often described as a maverick, Galbraith examined the character of the affluence and institutional changes through an objective intellect. More common at the time was the conceit of American exceptionalism, the pride of a nation which had won the war and now dominated the peace. That prosperity was based less on self-imagined American virtues than on the advantage of having an infrastructure intact and an industrial capacity left undamaged, as well as surviving as the sole financial superpower. This generation was later labeled "the Greatest Generation," (Brokaw, 1998) but most credit for their success is due their parents, whose pragmatism and ability to learn indeed rescued the nation and the world from a dark Depression and delivered it into a stable prosperity. This was the generation of Keynes, Keyserling and John Kenneth Galbraith.

Galbraith examined the rise of the corporation to dominance, the new centrality of government in the economy, and a new materialism that accompanied prosperity. His foundational book *The New Industrial State* defined the part of the economy dominated by the large corporations as the "Industrial System." (Galbraith J. K., 1967) Previously, corporations had ruled industries where scale of operations required bigness. Galbraith marked their invasion and occupation ever further into the economy. Today the pervasiveness of the corporation is even greater than when Galbraith wrote in 1967. It is now hard to find any sector, from groceries to coffee shops to farms to restaurants that is not the province of major corporations. *The New Industrial State* dissected the corporate culture, the technical reasons for its arising, the group think which he called the *Technostructure*, its goals, how it determined prices and controlled markets, and its ever more involved relationship with the state. Galbraith's writings explored a need for institutional counterweights to the corporate oligarchy — unions, governmental oversight, regulations, and social insurance.

Hyman Minsky and Financial Instability

Beginning with the administration of Richard Nixon, Demand Side began losing influence. (Although Nixon famously repeated the line, "*We're all Keynesians now.*"[1] With the ascension of Ronald Reagan to the presidency in 1981, Demand Side economics was well on its way out. The pre-Depression free market ideology returned, and along with it the free-wheeling financial markets that had created the imbalances of the 1920s. The sturdy growth rate that had trended up steadily from the end of World War II into the 1970s bent to half its slope. The long-term trend rate of unemployment doubled. Median income stagnated. The disparity between the rich and poor grew. The federal debt ballooned. The de-industrialization of America began. Aside from a respite during the eight-year Clinton Administration, that situation of underlying economic stagnation continued into the Great Recession. But the period after 1983 did witness a return to low inflation. Tepid growth and low inflation came to be known as "The Great Moderation." This was taken by the economic establishment to be stability.

Maverick economist Hyman P. Minsky, a practitioner of legitimate Keynesianism, identified this placid surface as the incubator of instability, an inherent characteristic of capitalism. Minsky published *John Maynard Keynes* in 1975, a treatment bringing Keynes past the Neoclassical diversion. (Minsky, 1975) His *Stabilizing an Unstable Economy* cemented the analysis. (Minsky, 1986) The subsequent history has produced the ratification of Minsky's thought, which held that increased financialization of the economy meant an increased instability. This was quite the reverse of the orthodox view and particularly that of Alan Greenspan, who had ascended to the chairmanship of the Federal Reserve in 1987. Even now, the lessons of Minsky are completely unknown to a wide range of policymakers and economic actors, and known only in caricature to others.

As curious as it may sound, money is invisible to much of modern economic analysis. Minsky's concern was money and financing. He identified three

---

[1] 1971, in announcing wage and price caps to curb inflation.

levels of financing investment — hedge, speculative and Ponzi financing. The last is not only inevitably unstable, but inevitably arrived at, a function of capitalists reaching for ever greater returns. This financial instability scenario was developed by Minsky in the 1970s, long before it played out in the real bubbles and busts of the 1990s and 2000s.

Other insights are described in the chapter devoted to him in this volume. Among them are:

- There is a direct line from budget deficits to corporate profits;

- Money is created not by the central bank, but by financial markets in facilitating investment and borrowing;

- Inflation can be useful as a means of escaping economic crises without banking breakdowns.

Joseph Stiglitz and Globalization

Not only did the poor get poorer in the United States in inflation-adjusted, or "real," terms beginning in the late 1970s, but the poor got poorer around the globe, particularly in Africa and Latin America. Some Asian economies did begin to develop, but others struggled. Remarkable successes were scored in China, Japan, South Korea, and elsewhere. Tragedies occurred in Africa and Latin America. The economic reefs found by these countries often followed their adoption of the charts of the free marketeers, encouraged or even mandated by the International Monetary Fund. "Neoliberalism" (as unfettered capital linked to reduced government is known in global circles) failed within the United States, but failed even better in undeveloped countries. Nations where Neoliberalism was employed fell extremely hard. This international rise and fall has been the context for the work of Joseph Stiglitz on Globalization.

Stiglitz was awarded the Nobel Prize in Economics in 2001 for work in asymmetrical information, which demonstrated the absence of free market efficiency. He won a second Nobel, a Peace Prize, in 2007, as a key member of the Intergovernmental Panel on Climate Change, which analyzed the impacts of high and rising levels of carbon in the atmosphere. Like Keynes, Keyserling, and the Galbraiths, Stiglitz contributed in public life as well, first as chair of the Council of Economic Advisers under Bill Clinton and later as chief economist to the World Bank. Two of his books *Globalization and Its Discontents* (Stiglitz J. E., 2002) and *Making Globalization Work* (Stiglitz J. E., 2006) describe the causes and conditions of developing economies stressed, exploited and then shackled by Western Neoliberal mandates. His book *Freefall* dissects the financial crisis of 2008 and its ramifications. (Stiglitz J. E., 2010)

James K. Galbraith and the Predator State

The relationship between the corporation and the state outlined by John Kenneth Galbraith in *The New Industrial State* evolved into predation. The institutions of the state itself — particularly those developed in the New Deal — were levered into supporting roles for, or simply looted by, the corporate oligarchy, particularly in health care and finance. Corporate oligarchs, in conspiracy with politicians, under a banner of small government and reduced regulation, exploited privileged and entrenched positions. This evolution was chronicled and analyzed by John Kenneth's son James K. Galbraith. The younger Galbraith's "predator state" analysis, explicit and prescriptive, earns him a place in this volume.

James K. Galbraith was also involved in public service, serving as the executive director of the Congressional Joint Economic Committee in the 1980s and earlier in a lead role in the drafting of the **Humphrey-Hawkins Full Employment Act**, an update and reform of the **1946 Full Employment Act**.

The so-called Reagan Revolution, with its slogans of deregulation and market efficiency, swept the corporate sponsors of Neoclassical economics into power inside and outside of government. Though their analysis was not disproven, the younger Galbraith and his Demand Side lineage could not withstand the political tide. Banks came to run the Treasury Department. Health insurers and Big Pharma rode to riches on Medicare and the health care system. Big Oil wrote the federal energy policy. The pattern repeated. Regulators became captives to the industries they were supposed to regulate, culminating under George W. Bush. The capture of democratic political institutions was dissected and its pathology described by James K. Galbraith in a piercing tome *The Predator State*. (Galbraith J. K., 2008) His remains the most coherent and forward-looking macroeconomic perspective extant.

George Soros and the Way Markets Work

Notwithstanding the Latin American debt crisis and consequent U.S. banking crisis of 1983, the stock market crash of 1987, the systemic failure of the Savings & Loan banks in the latter part of the 1980s, the collapse of hedge fund Long-Term Capital Management in 1998, the Asian currency meltdown of the same year, the dot.com bust of 1999-2000, the Argentine failure of 2002, and other violent financial market crises, confidence burgeoned in the efficiency and even prescience of the Market. The symbol of this trust in markets was the Federal Reserve and its legendary chairman Alan Greenspan.

George Soros operated within the financial sector and made his billions by practicing a theory directly counter to efficient market fundamentalism. Soros' thinking was founded on the concepts of fallibility, uncertainty and "reflexivity." The latter idea he described, in relation to financial markets, as the manner in which the market creates or changes the very objective evidence it is supposed to reflect.

Soros' wealth and philanthropy make him unique among the economists here, but his perspective is similar, as well as his active promotion of policies counter to market fundamentalism. His books *The New Paradigm for Financial Markets: The Credit Crisis of 2008 and What it Means* (Soros, 2008) and *The Crisis of Global Capitalism: Open Society Endangered* (Soros, 1998) identified ever larger bubbles being created out of consecutive financial crises. The thinking is parallel to that of Hyman Minsky. The primacy of uncertainty in his work is in direct line from Keynes.

Soros shares and epitomizes the belief of Demand Side economists that markets by themselves are inherently flawed. An economy devoted to the leadership of the market will be blind and unstable. At the same time, markets are inherently powerful in harnessing human energy and distributing goods and services. The conclusion is that markets need structure and oversight for competition to be fair and for imbalances to be kept in check. The tendency of money to flow to the powerful and ebb from the powerless, combined with the particular need for oversight, means an efficient market economy requires a strong political democracy.

Steve Keen and the Great Financial Crisis

Among the economists featured here, Steve Keen is arguably the most prescient, at least the most precisely correct in foreseeing the Great Financial Crisis, its dimensions and its causes. He won the Revere Prize from *Real World Economics Review* as the single economist who most accurately predicted the events of the latter half of the decade of the 2000s. His book *Debunking Economics* (Keen, 2001, 2012) and his papers on mathematical modeling and the credit accelerator unlock what has happened, why, and why the vast majority of economists got it wrong.

At this writing, Keen may also be among the least known of our economists. An Australian, originally trained in mathematics, his command of that discipline allowed him to deflate many of the core assumptions of Neoclassical economics, as well as the mathematical proofs they employ in describing human behavior. Econometrics is the idiosyncratic offshoot of mathematics that has developed over several decades in Economics departments, virtually in isolation from the mainstream of mathematical thought. Keen's computerized dynamic modeling in an accounting framework is light years ahead of the efforts of general equilibrium economists. He is in direct line from Minsky in financial Keynesianism. He has laid out the importance of private debt and the dynamics of money creation by way of credit.

The immense explosion of debt during the 1990s and 2000s is invisible to Neoclassical models. To Minsky and Keen it is at the core of the collapse and is still the basic drag which prevents recovery. Understanding this debt enables an understanding of the difficult and revolutionary measures needed to escape its gravitational pull.

Nouriel Roubini and Crisis Economics

"That which cannot be sustained will not be sustained." This sentiment or a variation has been attributed to many economists, but it is Nouriel Roubini in the modern day who most precisely identified what cannot be sustained and the time-line and scale of its fall. In the midst of a "Goldilocks Economy" (not too hot, not too cold; referred to previously as the "Great Moderation"), Roubini began talking about the Three Ugly Bears — a U.S. mortgage meltdown, the end of cheap credit, and higher oil prices — and a new and deep recession. His warnings were ignored until after the recession was underway. He then began predicting the financial meltdown that could emerge from the downturn. Again he was not believed until after the process was well underway. At this writing Roubini has identified the centripetal effect of imbalanced trade and excess debt in major European economies absent a restructuring of that debt. At this point, the consensus view is that no such action is advisable or practical.

Roubini's ruthless pursuit of analytical integrity and his repeated success in predictions while others fail are the reasons he is included here. This, and the fact that the subject matter of his work completes the historical range of our survey. Roubini's approach is best described as eclectic, rather than Demand Side. But his is an insider's view of the financial crisis. His book, *Crisis Economics* lays out the nut.

> **"For the past half century, academic economists, Wall Street traders, and everyone in between have been led astray by fairy tales about the wonders of unregulated markets and the limitless benefits of financial innovation. The crisis dealt a body blow to that belief system, but nothing has replaced it."**
>
> (Roubini & Mihm, 2010)

The increased financialization of the economy predicted by Minsky and witnessed over the decades since 1980 was accompanied by an increased search for yield, for higher returns on invested capital. As the yield from productive assets in the real economy declined, this search drove financial players to ever higher risks and to investments based on Ponzi returns — increases in asset prices — rather than productive returns. Often these risks were masked by exotic financial innovations. Mathematical risk allocation models purported to define risk in new ways that could be mitigated, but these were fundamentally flawed by unrealistic assumptions, limited historical perspective, or simply bad design. Risk was spread around the globe in the form of securities (packages of mortgages or other assets), and the exercise was assumed to have diluted that risk. Quite the opposite was the case. Often the components of securities (for example, the individual mortgages) bore much higher risk than was assumed for the total.

The innovations were successful as means of attracting investors' money to risks they did not fully understand (Stiglitz' asymmetric information problem). They were very successful in improving the short-term fee-based profits to banks. A flood of money soon glutted markets demanding more of this kind of return. Lending standards went down, and predatory practices and fraud went up. After the crash, as the flaws were exposed, securitization dried up. The Federal Reserve became the only buyer, bailing out the holders of more than $1.25 trillion in dodgy securities. The innovations became "legacy issues" for banks, threatening their solvency for years to come.

The sovereign debt crisis in Europe that appeared a few short years later was a legacy of the housing and financial meltdowns as well. When an early appetite for stimulus to the real economy faded, the private debt burdens, the banks' continued weakness and unwillingness to lend, and the imbalances in trade were exposed. When none of these problems was dealt with directly or firmly, weakness flowed onto national budgets and the financial casino went to work on sovereign debt. When the Market demanded austerity in the form of cutting government spending further, the downward demand spiral began and reinforced itself with each new austerity. Weakening economies offered even less prospect for servicing rising debt burdens.

Nouriel Roubini followed this from in front. His predictions were commonly met with derision, disagreement and dispute, but as the processes unfolded those responses melted into, if not agreement, at least silence. We employ his view as a window onto what will happen in the short- and intermediate-term futures.

Now we take each of these economists in turn, fleshing out their thought and the historical context in which they worked.

Chapter 4:

John Maynard Keynes and the Great Depression

Capitalism is the astounding belief that the most wickedest of men will do the most wickedest of things for the greatest good of everyone.

- John Maynard Keynes

Economics occurs in historical context. The two world wars and the intervening two decades was the context for British economist John Maynard Keynes' identification of the primacy of demand, the originating point of Demand Side. This period included a post-World War I inflation and slump. In the United States the economy rebounded into the Roaring Twenties. In Great Britain there was no rebound; the 1920s was a period of deep stagnation. The stock market crash of 1929 and the steep decline into Depression thus struck hard at America, but only deepened Britain's doldrums.

Keynes participated in public policy from the beginning. As a young Treasury official, he was chosen to assist in the negotiations at Versailles closing World War I. Before the treaty was concluded, he quit in disgust, and subsequently published his acerbic *The Economic Consequences of the Peace* in 1920. (Keynes, 1920) This short volume gained immediate and widespread attention. Keynes caricatured the august leaders gathered to decide the fate of Germany — Woodrow Wilson (United States), David Lloyd George (United Kingdom), Georges Clemenceau (France), and Vittorio Orlando (Italy). He laid bare the internal contradictions of the treaty's demands. Severe reparations were demanded from Germany, designed to keep that country weak. Keynes saw that the terms were arithmetically impossible and were certain to lead to instability and potentially to political volatility and backlash. Over the next decade and a half his analysis proved out. The desperate economic vise required to produce the reparations payments led to hyper-inflation and depression, followed by the social disruption that gave rise to Hitler and the Third Reich.

To the popular mind and to many of the intelligent and educated, the Great Depression foreshadowed, or even marked, the end of the capitalist experiment. Traditional economics had failed — failed to predict, failed to explain, failed to find a way out. The standard economics of the time did not include the possibility of the massive unemployment and industrial stagnation that fell upon the world. Previous crises were corrections in a long-term stable state, according to the dominant view. When Depression began, as it worsened, and as it lingered, the advice of economists was, "*Patience. Stay the course.*" Meanwhile, the successful economies in dealing with the crisis were those of new Nazi Germany and Stalinist Russia.

The Critique

The classical economists' perpetual denial was founded on Say's Law. This was the proposition that production itself, by its payments to labor and capital, created the precise amount of demand to purchase that production, or "*a product is no sooner created than it, from that instant, affords a market for other products to the full extent of its own value.*" (Say, 1803) Adherence to Say's Law was virtually a litmus test to be considered as a serious economist.

The experience of the real economy was quite different. Farmers produced milk, but dumped it in the street for want of buyers at a reasonable price. As prices crumbled, incomes crumbled, people hoarded against expected want, demand receded further, and the cycle went around again. Keynes saw that restoring adequate effective demand was the only route to the return of an economy which fully employed both its labor and capital. Demand could create production, but production did not necessarily create demand. When effective demand fell short, it was the proper role of government to step in with demand of its own, to employ people and return society to full production, which meant full employment.

Keynes postulated a "liquidity trap," which arose when people preferred hoarding cash to investing or purchasing. In fact, under conditions of uncertainty, and particularly when inflation turned to deflation, hoarding was an eminently sound practice, since cash became more valuable over time. Pairing Keynes' work with that of his contemporary Irving Fisher and adding the later work of Hyman Minsky unlocks the key concept of **debt deflation**. When assets are bought with borrowed money and then do not produce the income to service the debt incurred, they must be sold. Such sales, if widespread, produce downward pressure on asset prices. Foreclosure, bankruptcy and voluntary writedowns continue in a cycle which has no natural floor. Quite a different experience than the natural balance produced by Say's Law.

The Multiplier

In concert with its originator R.F. Kahn, Keynes developed and promoted the multiplier. The producer of one good is the consumer of another, as his good is sold and he spends his income. The same money buys shoes from the shoemaker as buys bread from the baker as buys meat from the butcher, but the consumer changes from shoemaker to baker to butcher. If the money stops, as above, in one or another's hoarding, the sequence of purchases and sales is interrupted and the employment of people and facilities down the line never occurs. On the other hand, new investment or government expenditure can create an economic surge as it echoes through the economy.

The quantification of this sequence is Kahn's multiplier.[1] Any particular amount of government spending or private investment will create multiples of that amount in economic activity as the money is passed from a consumer to a producer who then becomes the next consumer. The multiplier describes how much more activity will be created. It is the multiple of investment or government spending in increased real economic activity.

This concept has wide application. For example, the behavior of different economic actors will affect the multiplier differently. New income to a poor person will likely survive intact as a purchase of a good or service because a poor person tends to spend all of his or her income. Similarly, payments that go through government, because government is not in the business of saving, tend to employ people and survive as demand for the subsequent services. In contrast, payments to the wealthy are not so readily turned over. The tendency to save or spend in a manner which is tangential to the main economic life of the society is much greater among the wealthy. This means that simply transferring income from the wealthy to the poor or to government will increase economic activity. We look at this again later.

Today, popular use of the multiplier survives primarily as a way to describe the stimulus value of government deficits and to offer an (often inappro-

---

[1] Please note to avoid confusion, this "investment multiplier" is distinct from the *input-output multiplier* often used to gauge the effects of industrial development on the surrounding community or region. Keynes' multiplier is also distinct from the *money multiplier* which is essentially the action of the fractional reserve banking system in a healthy economy.

priate) justification for all tax cuts. Keynes himself preferred direct employment through public works.

Casino Markets

Like George Soros, considered later in this volume, Keynes was a successful investor. He made a fortune for his Cambridge college by speculating in futures markets, and financed the London arts community with his activities in markets. Also like Soros, Keynes was a relentless critic of the same markets:

> **"Speculators may do no harm as bubbles on a steady stream of enterprise. But the position is serious when enterprise becomes the bubble on a whirlpool of speculation. When the capital development of a country becomes a by-product of the activities of a casino, the job is likely to be ill-done."**
>
> (Keynes, 1936)

Needless to say, Keynes tirelessly promoted structure and regulation of markets. The financial regulations adopted during the New Deal and again after World War II were in his view essential measures to rebuild economies and the global system after World War II. These types of financial restrictions were replicated by governments throughout the world.

Keynes led a British delegation in 1944 to the Bretton Woods Conference in New Hampshire. Here the architecture of postwar economic arrangements was set. International financial bodies like the International Monetary Fund and World Bank were established. The British were in a very weak position in negotiations at Bretton Woods, being heavy debtors and deeply reliant on the U.S. Consequently the results of negotiations corresponded very closely to American interests. A dollar-centric fixed exchange rate scheme, for example, was imposed. This lasted only into the early 1970s. Keynes' *special drawing rights* alternative was not selected. SDRs were a complicated artificial money that would have served as an international reserve currency, facilitated support to developing countries and prevented the kinds of bias and trade distortions that are inherent in a floating exchange rate system. The American preference for debt and loans with terms was embodied in the IMF and World Bank. Later, particularly after 1980, these two institutions espoused ever more strict conditions for their loans. Now the IMF and World Bank directly coerce budget austerities, market-favoring reductions in government and privatization of economies. These are policies Keynes deplored.

To draw the point explicitly: The postwar economic prosperity was founded on financial markets that were tightly regulated, the casino that created the Great Crash had been silenced. This belief in structured and controlled financial markets is a major part of the Demand Side policy framework that was dismantled beginning in the late 1970s.

Keynesian Stimulus

Keynesian stimulus — deficit spending to support aggregate demand — was employed in the United States under the auspices of the New Deal. The goal was as much to alleviate want as to stimulate the economy, but the strategy worked on both accounts. The War validated the Keynesian prescription, as massive government expenditures and the employment of millions in the military and millions more in munitions and support supercharged the economy. The unprecedented output may have been dedicated to the nonproductive activity of war, but domestic standards of living also increased across the board during the War. People ate better, dressed better and lived better in the United States during the War than they had in the years prior. At the same time they generated the tremendous product the War consumed. The paucity of effective aggregate demand was replaced by an excess of demand.

NIPA and Simon Kuznets

Despite the whiplash change in the economic landscape from the stagnation of Depression to a supercharged economy, along with its wartime price and production controls, economists were not left in confusion, and in fact, directed activity efficiently. The prosecution and organization of the War were aided immensely by the ideas of Keynes. The National Income and Product Accounts (NIPA) were invaluable in managing war production. The prime mover in developing these accounts was Simon Kuznets (1901-1985) who operated directly out of the Keynesian playbook. NIPA's accounts and concepts for product, investment, income, and government activity are still the metrics we use to assess macroeconomic performance, in essentially the same form as Kuznets developed. During the war, they were indispensible in managing scarcity and preventing economic dislocations and black markets from undermining the war effort.[2] Today we likely

---

[2] Also important to the War's triumphant production was close oversight of contractors and suppliers, led by the Truman Committee, which itself was led by Senator Harry Truman.

need less crude measures of well-being, production and use, as well as accounts that describe depletion of resources and damage to the common natural systems. These are considered later in this volume. But the NIPA accounts served admirably in Depression, War and setting up the prosperity that followed the War.

What happened when peace resumed? When the War ended, many — including the prominent American Keynesians — feared and expected a return to depression, now burdened with an enormous national debt. That did not occur. We learn why when we take a closer look at the New Deal and one of its stalwarts.

Chapter 5:

Leon Keyserling and the Prosperity of Postwar America

If I wrote on the left wall the policies most needed for economic growth, and on the right wall I wrote the policies most needed for distributive justice, they'd come to the same thing. I have indicted the economists for never seeing this.

Leon Keyserling

With the election of Franklin Roosevelt in 1932, the political culture of Washington changed. Inauguration of the president occurred on March 4. A national bank holiday was imposed immediately, closing all banks while they were examined. Three-quarters soon reopened, certified as solvent, and billions of dollars flowed back into them. The **Securities Act** was passed in May and established the Securities and Exchange Commission. The **Glass-Steagall Act** was passed in June. It established the Federal Deposit Insurance Corporation and separated commercial banking from speculative investment banking. Also in June the Homeowners Loan Corporation was established to stabilize a housing crisis. It prevented the foreclosure of millions of homes by facilitating the write-down of mortgages and their conversion into longer terms at fixed rates. Some owners who could not qualify for the new mortgages were retained as renters until the property was salable. These measures stabilized the financial system.

Roosevelt's first one hundred days also included the Public Works Administration and Civilian Conservation Corps, which hired tens of thousands of unemployed and a panoply of other programs such as the **National Industrial Recovery Act**. Some of these were effective, some not. A Second New Deal arrived in 1935 which expanded those direct employment programs with the Works Projects Administration, but added new and important elements. The **Social**

Security Act set up retirement, disability, health, welfare and unemployment benefits. The National Labor Relations Act protected and empowered union activity and arguably shifted political and economic power for a generation.

The American economy responded immediately to the New Deal. Industrial production rebounded over 50 percent in the first four months and continued to grow to 1937. Unemployment dropped from 25 percent, and reached a low of 9 percent in 1937. Families receiving assistance grew to three-quarters of those in need. A move to balance the budget and rein in the New Deal passed Congress in 1937, reversing the government's pattern of investment, and the economy slid back downward substantially, to recover again with a return of aggressive policy. Then things changed completely with the advent of a new World War in 1941.

A chief draftsman of the PWA, NIRA and Wagner Act was Leon Keyserling, one of hundreds of young people attracted to Washington after the Roosevelt landslide of 1932. Keyserling is probably the least recognized figure among the nine featured here, but in many ways the most influential in terms of his stamp on public policy and on the arc of development of the U.S. economy. He was an early and influential staffer to a key member of Roosevelt's "Brain Trust" Rexford Tugwell (under whom he had studied economics at Columbia), to Senator Robert Wagner and in housing and agriculture bureaucracies. Later he crafted the signal piece of economic legislation in U.S. History, the **Full Employment Act of 1946**. He became an original member of the Council of Economic Advisers, and in 1949 became its chairman.[1]   Of all, Keyserling is probably the most influential person to ever hold the post. He was the economic voice of the Truman Administration, and the one most responsible for the trajectory of economic policy, from housing to foreign engagement and everywhere in between. Keyserling's devotion to Truman was profound.

> **"In all my dealings with Truman, he had the two most important characteristics of a President. First, he had absolute courage and decisiveness. And second ... he never considered the politics of Harry Truman when he was making what he regarded as a big decision in the interest of the country. He very much identified the interests of the country with the interests of the plain people."**
>
> (Keyserling, 1971)

---

[1] Keyserling replaced Edwin Nourse, the first CEA chair, an agricultural economist whose leadership led to Truman's famous exasperation: "Give me a one-handed economist! All my economists say, 'on one hand ... on the other.'" With Keyserling, Truman indeed had a one-handed economist. His evangelical style and commitment to growth, full employment and distributive justice found an essential advocate in the determined president.

War to Peace

The transition from a war economy to a peace economy began with a Keynesian commitment to full employment. This was embodied in the **Full Employment Act of 1946**. While the original guarantee of full employment was removed from the **Act** as it passed through a conservative Congress, the goals of "*maximum employment, production and purchasing power*" recognized the validity of the Demand Side analysis practiced by the New Deal and the Keynesian wartime managers. It recognized the power of government to produce economic outcomes. This was an idea that was unthinkable only two decades earlier. In 1978, the **Act** was revised to reinforce the purpose of government to guarantee full employment. The so-called **Humphrey-Hawkins Bill** was identical in theme to the original **Act**, and one of its prime movers was Leon Keyserling, thirty years older and out of government, but still in Washington and still promoting his vision for the economy.

The economic events of the immediate postwar period look to be speed bumps on the road to the prosperity that followed. They were much more. The world was faced with challenges similar to those that followed World War I, and similar policy choices would have likely led to similar results. Indeed, most economists — including Keynesians — expected a return to Depression. But different choices were made and different results obtained.

The combination of pent-up domestic demand and the existential needs of a broken Europe created the recipe for a demand-pull inflation. Prices went up because there was more demand than could be supplied by existing and constricted war-based industrial capacity. Agricultural products, in particular, were in tight supply and being bid up by the day. Farmers could withhold sale for a month and realize a ten percent increase in the price. The orthodox solution was to dampen demand by raising interest rates. Truman and Keyserling chose instead to allow the temporary inflation to expand supply. Prices in manufactures moderated over time. The speculation in agricultural commodities broke suddenly to the downside (and in time for Truman's re-election in 1948).

The return of eight million men and women from the armed services into the civilian labor force was met, again, with the expansion of production to meet domestic and international demand, but also with the GI Bill, which moved millions off employment lines and into school, and with the Marshall Plan, which rebuilt Europe with American products. These were "unaffordable" to the conservatives in Congress, but to the Demand Side paradigm and to the dedicated and capable bureaucracy that emerged from the New Deal and the war effort, they were eminently do-able.

Housing was favored by Keyserling and Truman as a social stabilizer as well as an employment engine. The construction of new housing increased the quality of life, but also generated employment to the skilled and unskilled and boosted related industries as well as public goods such as utilities and roads. Today's economy displays the result of a corporate takeover of the housing promotion facilities, a subject explored in the chapter *James K. Galbraith and the Predator State*.

The Truman Administration confronted the prospect of a hostile and expansionary Soviet Union. It was Keyserling's contribution to NSC-68, the secret memo laying out the threat and the policy of containment, that demonstrated the effort would not bankrupt the nation as the isolationists contended. It should be noted here, however, that national health insurance was a casualty of the cost of military expansion, particularly for the Korean War. Also instructive is that Truman financed the Korean War on budget, and his term in office is the sole example in postwar history of a president running a net budget surplus.

Economy as Partnership

Keyserling and his mentor Tugwell were Institutionalists. Keyserling had learned institutional economics under Tugwell at Columbia University before both moved into the New Deal government. The Institutionalist analysis was originated by Thorsten Veblen at the turn of the Twentieth Century. Its critique of the place of business and consumerism and the interplay of economic actors and inefficiencies of the contest between interest groups were never acknowledged by classical economics. Keyserling expressed his Institutionalism in a belief that the economy should be a partnership between Labor, Business and Government. Each needed the other. In the aftermath of the War, however, with both labor and business chafing under the controls of government, Keyserling's hope for cooperation was never widely shared, let alone realized. That being said, the industrial monopoly enjoyed by the U.S. relative to the rest of the world was fertile ground for wage gains, profit gains and trust in government.

First among the principles that organized Keyserling's thinking was the need for consistent long-term goals. Public policy was distracted too often, he thought, by short-term analysis and forecasting. Growth was not a good in itself, but needed guidance toward such priorities as housing, education, health and the environment.

Keyserling advocated a permanent public service employment program for those not employed elsewhere, a program which he estimated would serve about one million people. Full employment would be supported as well by social insurance such as unemployment compensation. In objection to the passage of the Nixon welfare program, Keyserling wrote in 1975, *"The ragbag of costly and grossly inadequate welfare programs should be replaced with limited but universal income supports."* (Keyserling, 1975) Such a program could be designed to expand and contract with the unemployment rate. Proportionate to the labor force, Keyserling's one million would today be three to four million, but keep in mind unemployment in the decades after World War II rarely rose above 6 percent. To mitigate higher unemployment, the program would have to be larger. This alternative to the welfare state later found a proponent in Hyman Minsky, and to this day in proponents like L. Randall Wray.

Fed

Perhaps most remembered today is Keyserling's vigorous and apparently Quixotic opposition to the independence and power of the Federal Reserve. This and his style of communication are both epitomized in the title of his 1980 book, ***Money, Credit and Interest Rates: Their Gross Mismanagement by the Federal Reserve System***. (Keyserling, 1980) The book is subtitled "***The Fed's assist to inflation, recession and injustice and the readily available remedies in the perspective of the whole economy***." Monetary policy ought to "*accord with the real economic growth needs required to restore maximum employment and production,*" he thought. Under the Fed, it did not.

The Federal Reserve is the nation's central bank. It was established in 1913 to stabilize a banking system prone to panics. (In a particularly severe threat, the Panic of 1907, J.P. Morgan acted as the central banker.) "Panics" and runs on banks are often described in terms of "liquidity". One definition of liquidity is the ability to sell an asset quickly without affecting its price. Housing, for example, would not be a liquid asset except in extreme booms, because it cannot be sold quickly. Stocks may become illiquid when they cannot be sold without driving down the price. In solving liquidity problems a central bank may serve as a buyer of assets, or more often, will lend to the bank using the asset as collateral.

Banking is the basis of the payment system, the means of transferring money, which include checks, credit cards, letters of credit. Commercial banking has traditionally been based on accepting short-term deposits and making longer-term loans to businesses and home-buyers. Its deposits serve as the basis for its lending, which may be ten, fifteen, or more, times greater than its reserves. [2] This fact often alarms those not familiar with fractional banking. Prior to the reforms

---

[2] The loans, of course, create money themselves, being deposits in the accounts of the borrowers, an issue we take up later with Hyman Minsky in the creation of money.

of the New Deal, speculative investment was also a part of banking. This was changed by the reforms of 1933 (later rescinded by Congress in 2000). When banks fail, the payment system fails, the deposits it holds are lost, its obligations to others ("counterparties") are abrogated and the failure spreads, since the financial system is an amazing web of interlocking credit arrangements. The real economy depends on the payment system and the commercial lending. Segregating and protecting these functions from the investment banking function is a way of protecting the real economy from the vagaries of speculation. Comingling these functions creates a much less stable system. Protecting all of them creates an enormous obligation for the government and taxpayers.

The structure of the Federal Reserve was also altered by the New Deal. The Federal Open Market Committee was created and other changes made to redress what was perceived to be inappropriate control of the Fed by its con-stituent banks. The private banks of each of twelve regions literally own the reserve bank of that region, being the shareholders. Although the reserve bank is not controlled by these owners in the same way a private corporation would be controlled, it has been the criticism — and was Keyserling's criticism — that the Fed sets policy that benefits the banking sector at the expense of other economic actors. At a minimum, the two parts of economic policy — fiscal (taxing and spending) and monetary — if not coordinated can lead to frustration or im-balances.

The Federal Reserve's web site assures us, "its [the Fed's] monetary policy decisions do not have to be approved by the President or anyone else in the executive or legislative branches of government..." (Federal Reserve) This effec-tively makes the Fed a fourth branch of government, with sole control of one-half of economic policy. This was not always so.

The "**Treasury Accord**" of 1951 is marked as the event which transferred the reins of monetary policy to the Fed. This occurred during Keyserling's tenure as the chief economist of the Truman Administration, but it was vigorously opposed by him. The Truman administration's public standing had deteriorated, with a virulent campaign against the president and the Democratic Party known as the "Mess in Washington" campaign. McCarthyism was on the rise. The shadows of the Korean War were deep. Popular disapproval of Truman's recall of General Douglass MacArthur was widespread.

Federal Reserve supporters today cite the **Treasury Accord** as a great moment. Keyserling characterized the event as betrayal by William McChesney Martin, who became the chief negotiator for the Treasury when its Secretary John Snyder was suddenly hospitalized. Six days after the Accord, Martin was selected as Fed Chairman. It was Truman's and Keyserling's belief that Martin would act to minimize Fed independence. Such was not Martin's intention. The unity of fiscal and monetary policy was lost. Keyserling estimated the resulting excess interest costs to all borrowers totaled $1.87 trillion in the period 1952-1979. Monetary policy conducted separately by the Fed "*is wrong.*" Keyserling said.

> **"No President from Wilson when the [Federal Reserve] Act was set up, through Roosevelt or Truman, including even Harding and Coolidge, dreamed you could have a free-wheeling Federal Reserve System independent of the Treasury and of the Government.**
>
> ...
>
> **"There has been really no President who has fully grasped the potential of the great, unified, consistent, long-range national economic policy of the kind we had during World War II."**
>
> (Keyserling, 1971)

Keyserling left government in 1952, but remained in Washington until his death in 1987 as a private consultant and public lobbyist. He remained a life-long advocate for government management of the economy in partnership with labor and business. The Institutionalist analysis reached a more complete and convincing development under the great economist John Kenneth Galbraith and continues today under James K. Galbraith, his son and intellectual heir. We turn first to the elder Galbraith.

Chapter 6:

John Kenneth Galbraith
and the Rise of the Industrial State

It is not the quantity of goods that matters, but the quality of life.

JKG

The most direct look at the structure and motivation and influence of corporations in the postwar economy was taken by John Kenneth Galbraith. Canadian
born, Galbraith, like Keynes, served in several responsible positions in the
government over an extended period of time. During World War II he was director
of the key Office of Price Administration and assigned the task of keeping the
nation's wartime shortages from leading to price gouging or inflation. Galbraith
then managed the post-mortem survey of Germany to assess the causes and
conditions which led to its defeat. (Summary Report, United States Strategic
Bombing Survey, 1945) The briefing documents from that effort offer rare insight
into some of the less than epic causes for the demise of the Third Reich. Galbraith
was active in the political campaigns of Adlai Stevenson and John F. Kennedy, to
whom he was a close advisor. Galbraith served as ambassador to India under
Kennedy.

Where Adam Smith's look at the economy of 1776 revealed a competitive
marketplace which determined price and output, income and investment,
Galbraith's view two hundred years later presented something quite different. If
only by three relatively straightforward postulates, Galbraith subverted the entire
foundation of the Neoclassical or free-market paradigm.

(1)   Income is a function of power, not value.

(2)   Corporations are run for the benefit of their managers, not the stockholders.

(3)   The contest between the corporation and the people through the state is the defining contest.

These are, again, institutional dynamics. It is an economy composed of actors, not impersonal mechanical processes. That an institutional framework is not more universally accepted and applied in economics is testament to the need for modern economists to be convenient to the powerful. In three volumes — *The Affluent Society*, *The New Industrial State*, and *Economics and the Public Purpose* — Galbraith consolidated his direct view and his alternative. Even in the 1960s and 1970s, when he wrote these works, Galbraith saw that corporate control of economic activity had spread from the major industries it had controlled at the opening of the Twentieth Century — railroading, steelmaking, petroleum, etc., where scale required bigness, to all corners of the society, from groceries to newspapers and media. At the same time, he saw that the ownership of corporations had been transferred from strong personalities at the helms of businesses they had built — the Rockefellers and Carnegies — to anonymous stockholders.

> **"[The] stockholder ... is a passive and functionless figure, remarkable only in his capacity to share, without effort or even without appreciable risk, in the gains from the growth by which the technostructure measures its success."**

Hence the corporation itself came to be run not for profit maximization to benefit its owners, but for the personal gain of its managers, for their purposes, whether pecuniary or simply prestige. Stockholders are needed only insofar as they can be persuaded to bid up the share price and thus the rationale for further escalation of payments to the corporate officers. Thus the long-term vision which correlated with interests of the majority of stockholders and gave common ground with government and labor was replaced by a short-term vision and by an appetite for bigness. Short-term gains allowed higher bonuses. Bigness gave managers bigger salaries than their peers and front row seats at prestigious events.

Corporate oligarchy pushed the free market to the periphery of the economy and then further. Simultaneously the market fundamentalist explanation for events was encouraged in the halls of economics. Thus it came to be that an explanation fit only for many suppliers, none of whom could affect price, came to be worn by huge multinationals who shared markets and crushed smaller competition. The free market was twisted to mean domination by the biggest players. Hardly free.

Rather than being determined by supply and demand, price is determined by the oligopoly, the "big business" responsible for the preponderance of economic activity, acting sometimes as a monopoly and other times in other characters. The product of the society, rather than being rationally determined by need, was determined to a large extent by the manipulation and persuasion of the corporation. This was in no small way a function of the affluence of the post-war years. As Galbraith said, "*No hungry man who is also sober can be persuaded to use his last dollar for anything but food,*" but in even modestly more affluent conditions consumers' "*economic behavior becomes in some measure malleable.*" And so from the corporate dominance arose the industries of persuasion, advertising, promotion and manipulation of the political process. At its end,

> **"The initiative in deciding what is to be produced comes not from the sovereign consumer who, through the market, issues the instructions that bend the productive mechanism to his ultimate will. Rather it comes from the great producing organization which reaches forward to control the markets that it is presumed to serve and, beyond, to bend the customer to its needs. And, in so doing, it deeply influences his values and beliefs."**

Writing in 1967, Galbraith noted that some sectors had not come under corporate dominance.

> **"Agriculture, truck mines, painting, musical composition, much writing, the professions, some vice, handicrafts, some retail trade and a large number of repairing, cleaning, refurbishing, cosmetic and other household and personal services are still in the province of the individual proprietor. Capital, advanced technology, complex organization, and the other hallmarks of what we have come ... to consider modern enterprise are limited or absent."**

Subsequently many of these industries have come under the domination of large corporations.

In Galbraith's terms, the industrial corporation is motivated (and even required for the sake of its own survival) to manipulate as much as possible. The immense magnitude of investment and capital and time required to develop and implement a technology imply a similar magnitude of loss in failure. One answer is to arrange for the state to absorb this enormous risk, as it does with military hardware. This manipulation of demand is in part a function of affluence.

> **"There is little doubt as to the ability of the industrial system to serve man's needs. As we have seen, it is able to manage them only because it serves them abundantly. It requires a mechanism for making men want what it provides. But this mechanism would not work — wants would not be subject to manipulation — had not these wants been dulled by sufficiency."**

But the control of appetite is not control of belief. In the latter endeavor, the corporation and the state come together to create an illusion, an illusion which insists on the excellence of the current regime and so obscures the true nature of the challenges the society must deal with.

> **"If we continue to believe that the goals of the industrial system — the expansion of output, the companion increase in consumption, technological advance, the public images that sustain it — are coordinated with life, then all of our lives will be in the service of these goals. What is consistent with these ends we shall have or be allowed; all else will be off limits.**
>
> **All other goals will be made to seem precious, unimportant or antisocial. We will be bound to the ends of the industrial system."**

Does it have to be that way? Galbraith, writing forty years ago, said:

> **"The future of the industrial system is not discussed partly because of the power it exercises over belief. It has succeeded, tacitly, in excluding the notion that it is a transitory, which would be to say that it is a somehow imperfect, phenomenon. But General Motors, General Electric and U.S. Steel are viewed as an ultimate achievement. One does not wonder where one is going if one is already there. Yet to suppose that the industrial system is a terminal phenomenon, is *per se*, implausible. It is itself the product ... of a vast and autonomous transformation.**
>
> **...**
>
> **"It would be strange were such a manifestation of so-**

cial dynamics to be now at an end. So to suggest is to deny
one of the philosophical tenets of the system itself ... that
change is the law of economic life."

The State

Galbraith thought he saw a convergence of the two dominant economic systems — the command economies of the Soviet Union and the industrial system of the West. "*The convergence between the two ostensibly different industrial systems occurs at all fundamental points.*" The state is needed by the capitalist system to provide adequate demand and smooth prices, he thought.

> "The industrial system has no inherent capacity for
> regulating total demand — for insuring a supply of purchas-
> ing power sufficient to acquire what it produces. So it relies
> on the state for this. At full employment there is no mech-
> anism for holding prices and wages stable."

And organizational autonomy was essential to communist industries to be efficient.

> "Large-scale organization also requires autonomy....
> Large and complex organizations can use diverse knowledge
> and talent and thus function effectively only if under their
> own authority."

Some might say that this convergence ended badly for the Soviet nations when they overshot, as free-market "shock therapy" administered as a stimulant created instead depression and an oligarchy worse than any in the West. More aptly it might be said that in both situations the state became the servant of elites, whose interests were not in efficiency or stability or general prosperity, but in personal wealth and power. The Soviet system was dismantled for the benefit of corrupt oligarchs. The U.S. system has captured the state by political means. The outcome for former Soviet peoples has been devastating bifurcation and a long-term decline. The outcome for the U.S. has been benign only by comparison, an impoverishment of the middle class and a wholesale degradation of public goods and services and a corruption of state functions. ("*Only the innocent reformer and the obtuse conservative imagine the state to be an instrument of change apart from the interests and aspirations of those who comprise it,*" wrote Galbraith in ***The New***

Industrial State. (Galbraith J. K., 1967)

Galbraith made much of the relationship of the corporation to the state, not limited to the manipulation of the political process and apparatus. He observed the exaggeration of the importance of industries in which the state guarantees demand — notably national defense and security. The technological sophistication developed by way of the military industrial complex is astounding. Its efficacy on the battlefield is unparalleled, but as repeated failures in foreign wars have demonstrated, its usefulness in achieving political ends is not impressive.

In fact, the industrial system, the large corporation, does not have to disappear for solutions to be put in place. But the state must free itself to act as the representative of long-term survival and rational economic actions.

> **"[The] expansion of public services that are not sponsored by the industrial system, the assertion of the aesthetic dimension of life, widened choice as between income and leisure, the emancipation of education require that the monopoly of the industrial system on social purpose be broken. This will not ... be welcomed by all.... But it is not inconsistent with the continued existence of that system."**

If other goals are strongly asserted, the industrial system will fall into its place as a detached and autonomous arm of the state, but responsive to the larger purposes of the society.

Chapter 7:

Hyman Minsky and the Rise of Economic Instability

A theory that denies what is happening can happen, and sees unfavorable events as the work of evil outside forces, rather than as the result of characteristics of the economic mechanism, may satisfy the politicians' need for a villain or scapegoat, but such a theory offers no useful guide to a solution of the problem. The existing standard body of economic theory — the so-called Neoclassical synthesis — may be an elegant logical structure, but it fails to explain how a financial crisis can emerge out of the normal functioning of the economy and why the economy of one period may be susceptible to crisis while that of another is not.

Hyman P. Minsky

No more powerful explication of economic thought has been propounded than that of Hyman Minsky. Relatively unknown during his lifetime, Minsky is the main line of Demand Side financial theory from Keynes. Today Minsky is known largely for the "Minsky Moment," that point in a financial bubble when debtors must begin to sell their assets to meet interest payments. In a way the Minsky Moment does epitomize Minsky's thought, since it brings into focus a critical point in the sequence of financing structures. We will discuss these in greater length later in this chapter.

But one of the most powerful lines of Minsky's thought derives from the work of Michal Kalecki (kah-les-key), a Polish economist from the era of Keynes and John Kenneth Galbraith. (It is reported that at the London School of Economics, Keynes' model was taught as the Keynes-Kalecki model.) Kalecki's assumptions were simple and plausible. His elegant equations and proofs built on sturdy assumptions opened up basic connections between prices, productivity, wages, profits and investment. Algebra is a mechanical logic and its proofs are logical proofs. Its assumptions are explicit. Contrast this with the use of calculus in economics. The latter, although complex and impressive in its precision, draws approximate conclusions founded on assumptions that are often never made explicit. Even their causal directions, i.e., which is the independent and which the dependent, is assumed. The closed system imagined is functional for thermodynamics, but is completely belied by economic reality.

Kelecki's most simple assumption is that workers consume all of their income. Of course, the assumption is not completely true, but it is more true than not, and is not fatal to the analysis when it deviates. Deviation, for example, in Neoclassical economics from the assumption that all firms are price takers is fatal to that analysis. In Rational Expectations, it is fatal if we assume that market participants, indeed all economic actors, are not imbued with economic omniscience. Kalecki's proofs showed that in an economy with small government and little trade, investment equals profits, or profits equal investment. Minsky took this and demonstrated the effects on price. Price is positively related to the wage rate and to the ratio of investment goods to consumer goods production and negatively related to labor productivity. (Minsky, 1986) It's a no-brainer that prices vary in the opposite direction as productivity, because productivity simply means producing more with the same labor. If wages are stable, prices should fall with a rise in productivity. One theory of wages is that they tend to go up with productivity, as workers are rewarded with increased output. Indeed, it is thought that productivity increases are the sources of wage increases. Thomas Palley's "alligator chart" disproves this theory, as wages in the U.S. have been stagnant for thirty years, even as productivity has increased apace. (Palley T. I., 2012)

The relationship of consumer goods to investment goods is quite instructive. The algebra shows what we might also derive from common sense. As investment goods are emphasized over consumer goods, the price of consumer goods tends to rise, because, basically, workers in both sectors are bidding for the output of the consumer goods sector. So when the ratio favors investment goods more, demand for consumer goods is higher and output is lower.

The implications are not all so common-sensical. As new investment goes up, so do prices, to produce a condition in which higher prices, higher investment and higher profits coexist. Since investment also connects positively with output and income, we can expect these three — output and income and prices — to be in the same virtuous soup (ameliorated only by productivity gains). This is inflation in the real economy.

Inflation in the financial economy is another question. Certainly the printing of money to pay for services is inflationary. But prices spiking in one or another commodity — oil, for example — may bleed through into a general price rise and be inflationary in a limited sense. The specific price — oil, corn, whatever — is only a price spike, since inflation is by definition a general phenomenon. In recent years we have seen commodities across the board rise and mimic inflation. (Demand Side suspects, at least on the non-food side, this may be a financial phenomenon of casino markets.) Inflation aside, a somewhat surprising empirical finding of our research on economic performance by president was that in the postwar period employment is higher, unemployment lower, investment higher, corporate profits higher and GDP growth better when a Democrat is in the White House.[1] This may seem counterintuitive when one considers the extensive efforts by Republicans to push companies into profitability via the tax code and deregulation. Kalecki and Minsky demonstrated why it has to be that actual profits do better under policies that favor demand over those which subsidize supply. Democrats, we suggest, what-ever their ideology or economic understanding, favor constituencies that increase demand, and so sometimes as a byproduct of policy, increase economic well-being for everyone.

Prices, Minsky says, carry profits, the *raison d'être* for investment. When government and taxes and deficits are introduced, something remarkable appears in Minsky's proofs. He shows that after-tax profits equal investment plus the government deficit. When there is no investment, profits equal the deficit. The enormous deficits following the Great Financial Crisis indeed empirically correlated with enormous profits in the absence of investment. One implication is certainly that business interests ought not now be concerned about deficits. They are supporting profits. Minsky produced extensive analyses of nesting cost curves, which we will not approach in this volume. Here we simply mention that financing constraints drive investment decisions on the Demand Side, as in the real world. In Neoclassical analysis, financing is invisible.[2]

---

[1] Research to appear in a forthcoming volume.

[2] Note here that Minsky's profit is not the same profit with which we are familiar. Minsky's profits he also terms the "surplus," and it is not only the return on capital we normally think of as profit, but all the returns which are not technologically determined costs of production. These include advertising and professional services, executive salaries and overhead costs, costs of financing and the aforementioned costs to validate capital assets. Profit or surplus feeds the white collars and presumably the big salaries as opposed to the blue collars on the production side. In addition, price-taking firms are disciplined into being more lean and less top heavy.

Recent concern over the approach of a "fiscal cliff" at the end of 2012, when a range of tax cuts expire and spending restrictions begin, demonstrates at least a latent understanding of the role of government deficits directly supporting the cash flows upon which corporate profits depend, as in Kalecki's algebra.

But let's go back to the price takers versus the price makers. What happens when demand falls? In the case of price takers, those who cannot affect the market or the price they get from the market, the Neoclassical price runs back along the marginal cost curve. In the case of price makers, who set the price and prevent its falling, something else happens.

If output drops below the first critical average cost curve, capital asset prices are no longer validated and investment in new capital assets stops. If output drops below the second critical curve, fixed debt payments can no longer be supported, and the various financing instruments come under pressure. Of course, the overhead and executive costs are compressed to some extent, but these may be resistant. For example, firms may increase advertising in attempts to influence demand. When overall demand affects many firms, the same kinds of financial instruments come under pressure and we walk into the Minsky Moment.

See that the deflation in prices is resisted by such firms on their products, because they have individual pricing power, but that the drop in output affects incomes and investments and financial arrangements dramatically. Since investment is affected, investment goods are affected, and they deflate in value. (The attempt to inflate asset prices by increasing the money supply does not touch real investment, but only liquid financial assets — stocks, bonds, derivatives.)

The most clear construction of Minsky's development of financial Keynesianism comes in his description of the three financing structures: **hedge, speculative** and **Ponzi** financing.

Hedge financing is what we think of when we think of investing in real assets. It is debt incurred which is designed to be paid off with revenue from the output of the investment. (John Kenneth Galbraith, remember, joined Minsky in pointing out that corporations are driven to attempt to control demand for large investment because they must have an extended stream of profits to justify large investment outlays.) Hedge financing is also seen in the thirty-year mortgage, which is an investment paid off by the rental value of living in the house.

Most basic treatments of microeconomics begin and end with fixed costs, variable costs, average costs and marginal costs. Prices are determined by marginal costs and where the marginal cost curve intersects the demand curve. This may be true, Minsky says, for price takers. But a whole great swath of the economy, including the dominant capital-intensive sectors, is composed of firms which more or less **set** prices and vary **output** according to demand. These firms operate on the basis of a set of nesting cost curves, the highest of which includes capital asset validation cost, or profits in the normal use of the word. Such firms keep **prices** at the requisite level when demand falls by their market power, pricing power. Without this ability to constrain price movements, they may not be able to employ expensive and highly specialized capital assets and large-scale debt financing, Minsky observes. So a control of the market that is not allowed in primitive economics is actually necessary in the practice of capitalism.

Speculative financing is interim and rollover financing. Everything from a strip mall to a huge industrial complex obtains construction financing, with the idea of refinancing upon completion. Speculative financing in the form of commercial paper, lines of credit, and a host of other innovations have made short-term credit ubiquitous in commerce. This was far more true prior to the Great Financial Crisis of 2008. Part of the destruction of money is a result of the drying up of this form of leverage or "intermediation." Much of the Federal Reserve's intervention in financial markets was, in fact, to prop up and even replace private sector speculative financing.

Ponzi financing. When borrowing is undertaken to purchase assets with the idea of capturing a gain in the price of that asset, this is called Ponzi financing. Bubbles are made of this. It is a self-reinforcing loop. As credit is extended to purchase assets, prices rise, profits are made, paper wealth increases regardless of any improvement in use of the property. The increased value seems to justify further purchases and even provides apparent collateral for further credit. But the price cannot go up forever. At some point credit is not extended. Since credit arrangements underpin the price, there is no facility for making these payments other than capturing price gains. When prices don't gain, the process begins in reverse and is self-reinforcing in the downward direction as well. The Minsky Moment, when assets must be sold to meet interest payments, leads to further price deterioration, which causes other Ponzi investors to sell. Credit again contracts, and another loop begins.

As investment activity declines from the peak of the bubble, so the economy declines. Formerly safe speculative investments can then become Ponzi. Rollover credit can disappear and more assets go on the market to meet debt payments. As the economy declines further, even hedge financing can come into question, as the long-term projections for returns fall with falling demand.

In financial crises prior to the 1950s, bankruptcies and bank failures purged the economy of the excess debt and credit. The economy typically shrank violently, but the crisis was eventually followed by the return of demand and investment, and a new expansion. Subsequent to World War II and the advent of big government, inflation came to accompany recessions. This had the effect of reducing debt service in real terms and sometimes maintaining the price of assets at nominal levels that did not require wholesale liquidation. In the period after the Great Financial Crisis, however, both processes were aborted. The Fed and Treasury acted to protect the banks, under the belief that they were too big to fail or under the illusion that the crisis was not a solvency issue, but a temporary problem of liquidity. It was thought that special facilities could keep the credit flowing and stabilize the prices at their Ponzi peak.

Minsky did not foresee such a policy tangent. He viewed the central bank as the lender of last resort and believed that inflationary monetary policy would prevent the real value of debt from coming over the top and thus the deflationary cycle from taking hold. Big government would support a base level of demand and keep the financial system from imploding completely. Inflation would make fixed debt payments relatively lower.

As we'll see when we visit the work of Steve Keen, the tremendous private debt that developed between 1990 and 2008, particularly in the years of the housing bubble, prevented any recovery. One result of the Great Financial Crisis was that sovereign debt expanded dramatically as this private debt was offloaded onto the state, and national governments struggled to unlock the frozen and dysfunctional financial sector. Early efforts at stimulus, to replace the sudden drop-off in consumer demand, were ridiculed when they did not quickly cure the sick economy and were subsequently abandoned in a paroxysm of austerity. Thus the degradation of tax revenues continued apace and deficits grew even in the absence of recovery spending. The sovereign debt issues attracted actors to a political sideshow, but the immense overhang of private debt began the crisis, and it was this private debt that prevented any meaningful recovery.

Minsky's work followed not only from Keynes, but from the economist Irving Fisher (1867-1947) who propounded the debt-deflation theory of the Great Depression. Here is Fisher's capsule of the downward self-reinforcing dynamics of depression and its behavioral and market responses:

> **According to the debt deflation theory, a sequence of effects of the debt bubble bursting occurs:**
>
> 1. **Debt liquidation and distress selling.**
> 2. **Contraction of the money supply as bank loans are paid off.**
> 3. **A fall in the level of asset prices.**
> 4. **A still greater fall in the net worth of businesses, precipitating bankruptcies.**
> 5. **A fall in profits.**
> 6. **A reduction in output, in trade and in employment.**
> 7. **Pessimism and loss of confidence.**
> 8. **Hoarding of money.**
> 9. **A fall in nominal interest rates and a rise in deflation adjusted interest rates.**

(Fisher, 1933)

Chapter 8:

James K. Galbraith and the Predator State

> *A governing myth hides an underlying reality, and any attempt to govern through the myth is bound to be short-lived. So it was with Reagan. But what is the essence of ... reality in the American case? If we do not actually live in a world made by Reagan, just as the Soviets did not actually live in a world made by Marx, what is the true nature of our actual existing world?*
>
> *An evolutionary economist knows where to look for the answer to such a question: at institutions.... The fundamental public institutions of American economic life were those created by public action in an earlier generation — by Franklin D. Roosevelt in the new Deal and World War II, by Lyndon Johnson in the Great Society, and to a degree by Richard Nixon.... These institutions have, to a large extent, survived to the present day.*
>
> *But if they have survived, obviously they have not survived undamaged.*

> **James K. Galbraith**

The son of and direct intellectual heir to John Kenneth Galbraith is James K. Galbraith. The younger Galbraith carried forward his father's interest in institutional structures, his respect for the work of the New Deal and perhaps most importantly his keen ability to take a direct look at economic events and build an interpretation of the economy quite at odds with the Neoclassical and market fundamentalist orthodoxy, but quite useful in unlocking actual economic events. His book, **The Predator State** examined how corporate capture of government allowed an exploitation of the institutions of the New Deal for private gain. The legitimate social agenda and public policy objectives of these institutions became distorted to divide profitable from unprofitable. The costly elements were assigned to government and the profitable diverted into private hands.

Galbraith came to Washington in the 1970s as a Congressional staffer and rose to the position of chief of staff to the Joint Economic Committee of the U.S. Congress, a function created by the **1946 Full Employment Act**. With the triumph of the Reagan Revolution in the early 1980s and the defeat of the liberal Demand Side agenda, Galbraith moved to the University of Texas, where he has taught for several decades.

Having worked on financial crises from the time of the rescue of New York City in 1975, Galbraith saw the events of 2008 as the biggest threat to the system as a whole since the late 1920s. Galbraith's analysis of the breakdown of the economy during the Bush presidency was early and accurate. *"This is the big one,"* he told Bill Moyers. (Galbraith J. K., 2008)   But he also saw the great advantage in 2008 over 1929, the fact that the New Deal had happened. The institutions of the New Deal, although they had been badly damaged, were still extant: deposit insurance, Social Security, a government capable of acting as lender of last resort, and with the capacity to borrow and spend as needed to deal with the crisis.

The wherewithal to handle the crisis existed in 2008. Lacking was a government willing to use that capacity. The way was open, with the collapse of the old objectivism of Alan Greenspan, for thinking afresh and clearly about the problems and how to solve them. Absent was the intellectual integrity to face the facts and deal with them. This failure has perhaps been the greatest for economics as a discipline and for the modern version of representative democracy as a governing regime. Orthodox thinkers clung to policy prescriptions long after the intellectual premises had crumbled under the weight of evidence. They did so either from a lack of imagination, or more likely, for the need to preserve decades of professional capital built on the failed paradigms.[1] The Great Financial Crisis was, according to Galbraith, the breakdown of an entire system — the failure of financial regulation and of supervision of the banking system. It had caused a collapse of trust between banks, who no longer knew whether their counterparties (their partners in the web of interlocking financial arrangements) were solvent, of

---

[1] So complete was the ideological sway of anti-regulation over policy-makers, that at the time of the collapse, the campaign of Republican nominee for president John McCain had designated former Senator Phil Gramm as his likely Treasury Secretary. Gramm was the deep architect of the unregulated speculative markets that had collapsed.

trust with customers, who no longer trusted the banking system, and of trust with potential commercial borrowers.

In the midst of the maelstrom Galbraith presciently worried about the periphery of Europe and accurately prescribed the need to move quickly from rescuing the financial sector to rebuilding the real economy. Deficits were sure to rise to another level, he said. They would rise either because nations supported employment by public spending or they would rise because tax revenues would collapse with the collapse in that spending and employment.

Deficits were to be welcomed for filling the gulf created by the financial collapse. Deficits were even a good deal so long as interest rates were low.[2] The move Galbraith contemplated — a quick, clean rescue of the financial sector, then a robust rebuilding of the real economy — did not occur. In the aftermath of the crisis the rescue of the financial sector was enthusiastically executed in the U.S. by the Treasury and the Fed, under both presidents George W. Bush and Barack Obama. The chosen approach was instead a muddy "muddle through" strategy — not restructuring and reform, but bailout and backstopping. Bad practices survived. "Too big to fail" banks became larger. Smaller banks were allowed to fail. Unregulated securities, including private contracts such as credit default swaps, were made good by public interventions.

A financial reform measure, the **Dodd–Frank Wall Street Reform and Consumer Protection Act**, made changes around the edges, but substantially failed to alter practices in the casino markets or significantly amend incentive structures. Even these modest reforms were eroded in the back offices of regulators after the fact by an army of financial sector lobbyists. A consumer protection office, the Bureau of Consumer Financial Protection, was delayed by unprecedented Congressional maneuvering, again sponsored and abetted by financial sector money.

Meanwhile, the real (non-financial) economy received ill-designed stimulus. Under George W. Bush, the **Economic Stimulus Act of 2008** attempted to deal with the recessionary pressures using tax cuts and rebates. A 2009 measure under Barack Obama, the **American Recovery and Reinvestment Act** (ARRA) was much larger, but its $700 billion was divided roughly in thirds: (1) effective public works programs and supports to states, (2) relatively ineffective middle class tax reductions, and (3) the politically necessary but entirely ineffective tax concessions to businesses. The Bush 2008 measure followed largely on the

---

[2] Galbraith was later to embrace the nearly complete freedom of the federal government to spend as needed, the absence of a budget constraint. Government is at the center of money. Or more rightly, government can produce acceptable, secure accounts at will, whether cash or interest-bearing bonds. This line of reasoning, sometimes called Modern Monetary Theory, was developed by L. Randall Wray, et al.

"timely, targeted and temporary" template advocated by former Clinton aide Lawrence Summers. Summers became Obama's chief economic adviser in time to form the size and style of the 2009 ARRA.

The New Deal had established unemployment insurance, which was a large part of the effective federal support to the declining economy. But direct government jobs programs and the direct write-down of mortgage debt were examples from the New Deal that were ignored. Massive foreclosures beset the American household sector, but despite early signals by federal authorities that renegotiation of principle would be facilitated (as was the model set in the 1930s by the New Deal's Home Owners Loan Corporation), the sequence of measures trotted out by the Treasury and supported by the Administration failed to address principle. For both households and the holders of their mortgages, the chosen method was "extend and pretend." Extend terms and pretend the loans were good. The paper solvency of the big banks depended on their ability to carry bad loans on their books at full value.[3] Nor were the homeowners most in need able to take advantage of falling mortgage rates to refinance. As their houses fell in value, loan terms became more strict. Their equity had been wiped out, and equity was required to secure new mortgages. Housing and employment continued in deep recession, even as a nominal recovery occurred.

In his work outlining the capture and exploitation of government institutions by the corporate oligarchy, Galbraith identified a set of motives:

> **"[The] people who took over the government were not interested in reducing the government and having a small government, the conservative principle. They were interested in using these great institutions for private benefit, to place them in the control of their friends and to put them to the use of their clients. They wanted to privatize Social Security. They created a Medicare drug benefit in such a way as to create the maximum profit for pharmaceutical companies.**
>
> **"They used trade agreements to extend patent pro-**

---

[3] Very instructive was the discrepancy between how banks handled writedowns for mortgages on their own accounts vs. how they handled those acquired in acquisitions. For example, when Wells Fargo assumed the business activities of Wachovia, the loans of the acquired bank were reduced to market value in the process. Mortgage borrowers subsequently found letters in their mailboxes offering to cut principle owed to reflect reductions in values. Borrowers with loans held by the parent bank were not offered such deals. "Extend and pretend," was a practical measure to protect the balance sheet of the latter from reality. Since it was not necessary in the former case, the banks moved to practical loan management.

tections for various interests or to promote the expansion of the corporate agriculture's markets in the third world. A whole range of things that were basically political and clientelistic. That's the predator state."

The governing regime, Galbraith said, had become a "corporate republic," the purpose of which was to divert wealth from the public to the private sector.

"They ... turned over the regulatory apparatus to the regulated industries. They turned over the henhouse to the foxes in every single case. That is the source of the decline in and the abandonment of environmental responsibility, the source of the collapse of consumer protection, and the source of the collapse of the financial system, all trace back to a common root, which is the failure to maintain a public sector that works in the public interest, that provides discipline and standards, a framework within which the private sector can operate and compete. That's been abandoned."

The aftermath of the Great Financial Crisis was not a return to rational regulation and the enactment of New Deal style support to the real economy. The model of the New Deal would have led to straightforward programs: direct employment projects, mortgage principle renegotiation, clear and simple reregulation and federal support to states and municipalities. Instead, the financial and economic collapse was absorbed by the public sector, with the idea that relieving the financial sector of the weight of its error would allow it to turn to normal credit creation. Support to the banks, it was thought, would be multiplied by its lending. The government money would be amplified by a rejuvenated financial sector.

Bailouts and supply side tax concessions multiplied corporate profits, but did not increase employment. The deficits which followed from absorbing a recession brought on by private market excess were cited as evidence of government profligacy, even as those massive deficits stemmed the freefall and allowed a weak and halting recovery. And amazingly, out of the stagnation arose calls for precisely the deregulation policies that had led to the crisis. Thomas Palley was to call it the *"Neoliberal Two-Step,"* where conservative, market fundamentalism led to a breakdown that was itself the excuse for more conservative, market fundamentalist policy. (Palley T. , 2010)

The panic period of the Great Financial Crisis was papered over by the facilities of the Fed, above and beyond the official deficits incurred on budget. The

Fed absorbed trillions in mortgage-backed securities and backstopped virtually every private financial market. But when the panic ebbed, so did resolve to stabilize and protect the economy from financial markets. No effective reregulation occurred. Criminal prosecution was literally nonexistent, although criminal behavior was rampant at every level of the housing debt bubble. Fraud at mortgage origination extended to fraud at the level of design and sale of mortgage securities. No doubt the fraud was enabled by a near universal mania to buy and to borrow at any price. The panic of the collapse was muted by massive bailouts to banks and securities holders. Assurances were solemnly given that once the troubled ship was righted, the economy would resume.

Those assurances began to fade as soon as they were offered. They then disappeared from memory, as month after month, year after year, the recovery of the real economy — the object of the largesse to the financial sector — did not occur in any meaningful way. By the end of the decade, speculative finance was back in vogue, commodities and equities markets were floating on Fed-sponsored liquidity, banks were cash rich, their balance sheets were as opaque as ever, and the real economy toiled on under an ever-heavier load of debt. Galbraith turned from hopeful advocacy for the rebuilding of a sound public sector to discouraged defense against a new conservative assault on New Deal institutions, particularly Social Security. There would be no new economy engaged in rebuilding its infrastructure base or advancing to meet the challenges of climate change,

At issue was the size of the federal deficit. Although it is difficult to imagine the American economy yielding any positive news without impetus provided by the massive federal deficit, the conservative view was that the deficits that rose in the wake of the financial collapse actually caused the downturn and threatened the future. The prescription was austerity.

Galbraith assessed the economic contraction and its effect on the federal budget deficit and debt from the Demand Side. The deficit would grow, he said, no matter what policy prescription was followed. If government spent on infrastructure, jobs programs, or transfers to state and local government, the deficit would rise in support of economic stabilization and growth. If government reduced spending, cut services and ignored cash-strapped states, deficits would grow because of declining tax revenues and increased payments for unemployment insurance and other safety net programs. The latter process came with sagging employment and increased fragility.

Galbraith saw it to be the duty of government to step into the gap between the economy's potential and the declining output of the private sector. Borrowing rates had dropped to historic lows in spite of Fed zero rate policy designed to spur investment. Borrowing and investing were suddenly and dramatically out of favor.

Counter to Galbraith's perspective was alarm over the trajectory of the public debt fomented from many sides. The proposition that increasing deficits would lead to unsustainable economics was given currency by two prominent economists, Kenneth Rogoff and Carmen Reinhardt in the book *This Time is Different*. (Rogoff & Reinhardt, 2009)   The mocking title of the book and its portrayal of a historic pattern of deficits and decline following financial crises suggested that decline might be avoided if only profligate government reduced its borrowing and deficits did not reach a critical level, identified as 90 percent of GDP.

The Rogoff-Reinhardt analysis seemed to give credibility to budget hawks. Immediate crisis was conflated with long-term budget deterioration. Committees such as the Simpson-Bowles Commission, convened by Obama, and the bi-partisan Congressional Joint Commission on Deficit Reduction raised the volume on long-term budget balancing. Virtually all conversation was heavy on spending reductions and light on revenue enhancement. Galbraith's proposition that deficits would not be avoided, but could be constructive or not, was drowned out and not engaged.

Figure 8-1

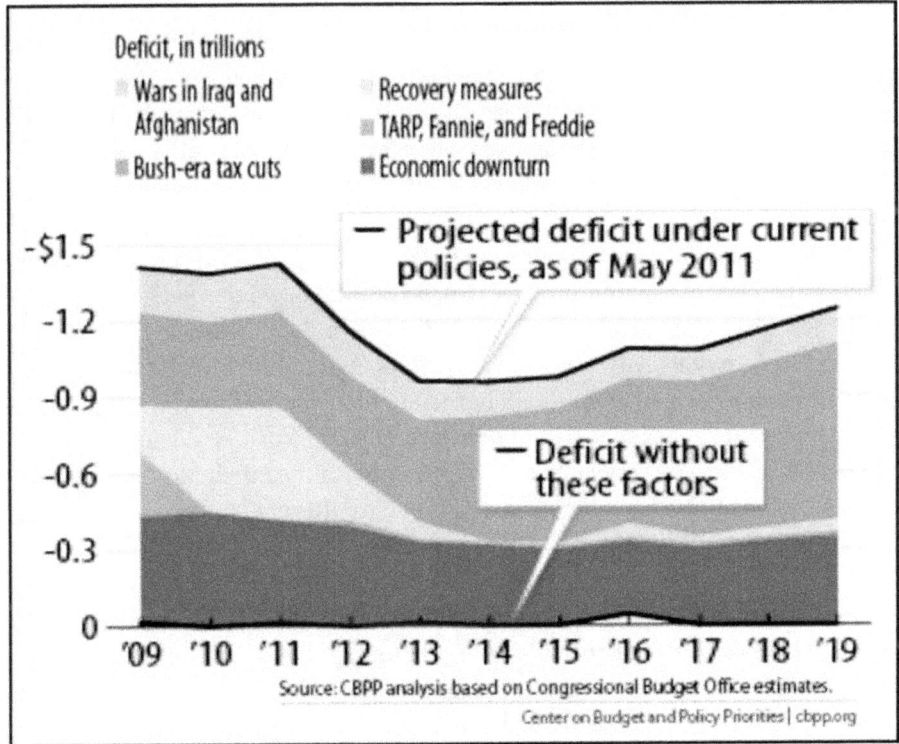

Deficit, in trillions
Wars in Iraq and Afghanistan
Bush-era tax cuts
Recovery measures
TARP, Fannie, and Freddie
Economic downturn

— Projected deficit under current policies, as of May 2011

— Deficit without these factors

Source: CBPP analysis based on Congressional Budget Office estimates.
Center on Budget and Policy Priorities | cbpp.org

The entirety of the deficits, actual and projected, can be laid at the feet of these causes:

- Military adventures in Iraq and Afghanistan,
- The Bush tax cuts of 2001 and 2003,
- The recovery measures of 2008 and 2009,
- Aid to the financial system as a result of the 2008 crisis,
- The effects on revenue and expenditures of the recession.

Absent these elements, the budget was in balance. Yet the objects of most fevered attention have been Social Security and Medicare. Figure 8-1, a product of the Center on Budget and Policy Priorities, breaks out the deficit by cause.

At the other end, looking forward to the future, Galbraith pointed out that the projections for deficits derived from Congressional Budget Office models contained internally contradictory assumptions regarding interest rates and inflation. (Galbraith J. K., 2010)   Specifically, the CBO's assumptions for interest rates on the debt were consistent with growth, inflation and revenue rates above those used in its analysis. As long as the economy remained stagnant, debt service would not expand to the degree envisioned and the deficit would remain below the CBO's projections.

The political agenda shaped the economic debate and determined the ground on which it was conducted. Republican intransigence on taxes married with Democratic eagerness to appear fiscally responsible. A series of episodes involving the previously symbolic exercise of raising the allowable level of debt exposed a political theater in Congress in which both parties appeared reckless and incompetent.

The issue of sovereign debt was inflamed by Rogoff-Reinhardt, but it only obscured the central issue of debt — that private financial markets had doubled private debt over the decade prior to 2007 through Ponzi financing. Then when the tide ebbed carrying with it trillions of dollars in household wealth and millions of construction jobs, it left the leaden burden of the debt behind it. Asset prices — notably real estate — fell. The debt that had run up those prices did not fall.

But we do a disservice to Galbraith's important contribution if we leave it to be distracted by the Great Financial Crisis and its aftermath.

> *predation*: **the systematic abuse of public institutions for private profit, or equivalently, the systematic undermining of public protections for the benefit of private clients. ... [The] practice of turning regulatory agencies over to business lobbies, the privatization of national security and the attempted privatization of Social Security, the design of initi-**

atives in Medicare to benefit drug companies, and trade
agreements to benefit corporate agriculture at the expense
of subsistence farmers in the Third World. In each case, what
we see is not, in fact, a principled conservative's drive to
minimize the state. It is a predator's drive to divert public
resources to clients and friends.

(Galbraith J. K., 2008)

While it is certainly regulatory capture on a grand scale, Galbraith's predator state is more insidious, or at least more complete. New Deal institutions
rescued capitalism from itself by mitigating instability and excess. A principled, if
badly flawed, conservatism under Ronald Reagan provided a cover for the rise of
the predator state under George W. Bush. Our new and present condition is without principle in the broad sense. Its virtue is an untested assumption.

In addition, Galbraith has done important work at the University of Texas
Inequality Project on inequality and its effects on people and their movement. His
2012 book *Inequality and Instability: A Study of the World Economy Just Before
the Great Crisis* demonstrated the connection between income equality and
prosperity. (Galbraith J. K., 2012)

His macroeconomic prescriptions demonstrate a depth of thought not
captured in our short chapter:

First, because markets cannot and do not think
ahead, the United States needs a capacity to plan. To build
such a capacity, we must first of all overcome our taboo
against planning...

Second, the setting of wages and the control of the
distribution of pay and incomes is a social, and not a market,
decision. It is not the case that technology dictates what people are worth and should be paid. Rather, society decides
what the distribution of pay should be, and technology adjusts to that configuration... And more egalitarian standards
— those that lead to a more just society — also promote the
most rapid and effective forms of technological change, so
that there is no trade-off, in a properly designed economic
policy, between efficiency and fairness.

Third ... the United States needs to come to grips with
its position in the global economy and prepare for the day
when the unlimited privilege of issuing never-to-be-paid
chits to the rest of the world may come to an end. We should

not hasten that day; in fact, if possible, we should delay it. We should take reasonable steps to try to keep the current system intact. But given the rot in the system, we should also be prepared for a crisis that could come up very fast. The fate of the country, and indeed the security and prosperity of the entire world, could depend on whether we are able to deal with such a crisis once it starts.

(Galbraith J. K., 2008)

Economist Joseph Stiglitz concurs.

My concern is that we have set in motion an adverse economics and an adverse politics. A lot of American inequality is caused by rent-seeking:[4] Monopolies, military spending, procurement, extractive industries, drugs. We have some economic sectors that are very good, but we also have a lot of parasites... [There] is always the risk that the parasites will devour the healthy body parts. The jury is still out on that.

(Stiglitz J. , 2012)

Now let us follow Stiglitz from domestic to international economics.

---

[4] Wikipedia: The simplest definition of *rent seeking* is to expend resources in order to gain wealth by increasing one's share of currently existing wealth instead of trying to create wealth. Since resources are expended but no new wealth is created, the net effect of rent-seeking is to reduce total social wealth. ... Profit-seeking is the creation of wealth, while rent-seeking is the use of social institutions such as the power of government to redistribute wealth.

Chapter 9:

Joseph Stiglitz and Globalization

> *Economics has been driving globalization, especially through the lowering of communication and transportation costs. But politics has shaped it. The rules of the game have been largely set by the advanced industrial countries — and particularly by special interests within those countries — and not surprisingly, they have shaped globalization to further their own interests. They have not sought to create a fair set of rules, let alone a set of rules that would promote the well-being of those in the poorest countries of the world.*
>
> **Joseph E. Stiglitz**

A recipient of the 2001 Nobel Prize in economics for his work on "asymmetric information," demonstrating the fallacy of market efficiency, Joseph Stiglitz arguably won a second Nobel in 2007 for his work with the Inter-governmental Panel on Climate Change, which received a Nobel peace prize. Earlier in his career, Stiglitz served as chair of the Council of Economic Advisers under president Bill Clinton and later chief economist at the World Bank. These positions within the institutions which guide international trade and development policy made his two books — *Globalization and Its Discontents* and *Making Globalization Work* — authoritative and thus their judgment all the more telling.

Later we will take up the problem of accounting accurately for output, income, resource depletion and so on. In this we will recognize his work with the Sarkozy Commission (formally "*The Commission on the Measurement of Economic Performance and Social Progress*" (Stiglitz J. E., 2009))

This chapter is our look at globalization and free trade, in practice and in theory. *Globalization* is a term for the coming together of the world economically, the integration of the world's economies. It has been described in some places as inevitable but benign, elsewhere as lethal. Trade between peoples and nations has been around for as long as people could travel, nearly as long as humankind. As the means of transportation became less expensive and more reliable, trade grew. Now trade has grown again. New industrial nations have risen in Asia founded on export. Trade now includes services as well as goods. But increased trade is not all that is meant by Globalization. Explicit in the new globalization is the free flow of capital and the opening and integration of markets. And while "trade" denotes an exchange, the current phenomenon is one of arbitrage of labor, regulation, currencies and financial instruments.

Arbitrage is taking advantage of the price differences between two or more markets. Financial arbitrage involves taking advantage of tiny differences in interest rates, exchange rates, spot and futures prices, or any other differences that can be found, buying in one market and selling in another. Financial arbitrage accounts for a tremendous proportion of the volume of financial transactions.[1] Labor arbitrage refers to exploitation differences in wage rates (adjusted for productivity) by moving operations, notably to the country with the lowest wages per unit of output. Regulatory arbitrage indicates the tendency to move activities to jurisdictions with the least onerous restrictions.

The model that originally described the gains to be expected from trade was developed in the 19th Century by British economist David Ricardo (1772-1823). It is based on the concept of *comparative advantage*. Where one country might have a comparative advantage in wine and another in wool, it benefits both parties to trade. "Comparative" signifies other than absolute. For example, if country A can make 8 gallons of wine or raise one sheep and country B can make only 4 gallons of wine per sheep, it doesn't really matter if "A" can make 100 gallons per man and "B" only 20. The benefit exists to trade sheep (or wool) for wine. No matter the relative level of prosperity, if we can get more wine by growing sheep and trading wool for it than by growing grapes and producing it ourselves, we are better off to do so. Ricardo's principle of comparative advantage and win-win from trade has the precision of the hypothetical. Ricardo's analysis occurred in the historical context of trade between relative equals, but also in the context of the British Empire. In the hypothetical world of comparative advantage,

---

[1] Taxing and reducing the volume of these financial transactions was the object of James Tobin and the "Tobin Tax." Tobin proposed in 1972 a minute tax on financial transactions that would be virtually invisible to the activity of the real economy, but would be significant to speculative activity because of its volume. (Tobin, 1972) Currency trading alone accounts for trillions of dollars per week in activity.

British Colonialism and Imperialism were conveniently ignored. The real faces of trade and Globalization both then and now are more apparent if we remember Galbraith's insight, that income is a function of power, not value. Just as in Ricardo's time, today we witness the domination of one people by another for economic benefit. Were Ricardo's model accurately reflected today, the well-being of all peoples would improve, general prosperity would improve. Although the issue is clouded by an enormous increase in the world's population, it is apparent that poverty has expanded and the disparity between rich and poor — nations and individuals — has expanded.

Trade today revolves more around the advantages of arbitrage than any real comparative advantage. *Competitiveness* is a word that is often used to describe the positions of nations. This usually means its place on the ladder of unit-labor costs, regulation, or exchange rates. Obviously the more free the movement of capital, the smaller the differences need to be that yield a profit. In any event, the practice of Globalization often involves gains based not on comparative advantage, but on control and exploitation of the exchange. It is no longer the vintner nor the shepherd who is better off, but the one who arranges siting of production and the transport of their goods. The returns from trade possible for the well-being of the broad society have been captured by the businesses which sponsor the trade, who also dominate the suppliers and control the distribution.

Pareto efficiency is an economic concept that is needed to justify trade from an efficiency standpoint. It was developed in the work of Vilfredo Pareto (1848-1923). If a net gain is possible, the activity is determined to be efficient. If one person *can* be made better off without reducing the lot of others, the process is determined to be *Pareto* efficient. *Can* and *will* are two different words. Their difference means that the efficiency has nothing to say about distribution. So if one person is made ten times better off and nine people are made worse off, but the net is positive, the operation is considered efficient. It is often said in economics textbooks, that gains *could* be distributed to make nobody worse off and at least one person better off. In practice, neither gains nor losses are typically shared.

For example, there is no doubt that many prices for consumers within the United States have been suppressed as a result of Globalization. The consumer is better off, but cheap imported manufactured goods have meant the loss of manufacturing jobs, many of which were held by those same consumers. Thus, trade agreements have been a target for the displeasure of labor unions and others because the costs have manifested in lower wages and loss of the manufacturing base, with the related loss of jobs.

The benefits have manifested in higher corporate profits and in lower consumer prices. The net positive impact of freer trade undoubtedly available in theory is in practice frustrated because the gains have not been shared with the natural losers, but monopolized by the corporate sponsors. The consuming public objects silently, if at all, to the outsourcing of jobs even as it fills the parking lots at Wal-Mart to buy the cheap Chinese goods.

The word "trade" denotes an exchange of goods or commodities. The currency of a country is simply the medium of exchange, eliminating the need for direct barter. If there is a difference in the volume of traded goods — imports and exports — and currencies are free to float, the currencies will adjust to each other to equalize the values. "Trade" means trade of goods for goods through the medium of currency. Long-term and chronic trade deficits such as the United States has experienced over the decades after 1980 amount to a failure of free trade theory. Currencies have not adjusted.

It is, in fact, the ambition of modern nations to be net exporters of goods, and importers of wealth. Here money becomes the store of value, not the medium of exchange. This is not new. The great wealth of Spain after its colonization of the Americas derived from its access to the money of the time — gold — both the medium of exchange and the store of value. Fast forwarding to the 21st Century, the U.S. dollar has become the "reserve currency," the store of value *and* the medium of exchange, for everything from hostage payments in Latin America to drug traffic in Central Asia, not to mention the usual business of trade.

Nations very often accept dollars as payment with the purpose of holding them, not of returning them for goods. When those nations then buy the bonds of the U.S. with the dollars, they are simply exchanging one form of liquidity for another that pays interest. This purchase is a simple matter of maximizing finan-cial assets. The discomfort over this debt, and even the occasional call to end the practice, ignores the reality that this is a simple outcome of unbalanced trade and eagerness for currency.

This is not to say debt is not involved. It is central. If you look at a dollar bill, you will see "*Federal Reserve Note*" at the top. What is the value of the note? Lower on the same side, the bill reads "*This note is legal tender for all debts, public and private.*" The currency is rightly identified as credit-money.

More could be said, but our point here is that massive trade imbalances which have characterized the U.S. economy since the 1980s have been incurred as a result of the place of the dollar as a store of value, as wealth in itself, and the eagerness of nations to accumulate wealth in that form. The simultaneous growth of "external debt" — that debt owed to entities outside the U.S. — is an accounting for this fact.

The economy can be conceived as composed of three sectors: household, business and government. So long as the household and business sectors are not significantly indebted, or if their debts are owed to each other — and by nothing more sinister than an accounting identity — the trade deficit and the government

Figure 9-1

Current Account Balance - 2012					
Rank	Country	Surplus (Deficit)	Rank	Country	Surplus (Deficit)
1	China	$305,400,000,000	180	Belarus	($8,500,000,000)
2	Germany	$188,400,000,000	181	Colombia	($8,943,000,000)
3	Japan	$166,500,000,000	182	South Africa	($9,987,000,000)
4	Russia	$71,130,000,000	183	European Union	($11,070,000,000)
5	Switzerland	$70,360,000,000	184	Vietnam	($12,220,000,000)
6	Saudi Arabia	$70,100,000,000	185	Poland	($15,900,000,000)
7	Netherlands	$60,090,000,000	186	Greece	($19,890,000,000)
8	Norway	$53,460,000,000	187	Portugal	($22,610,000,000)
9	Singapore	$46,270,000,000	188	Australia	($30,400,000,000)
10	Kuwait	$43,140,000,000	189	Brazil	($47,360,000,000)
11	Taiwan	$40,620,000,000	190	Turkey	($48,420,000,000)
12	Korea, South	$36,350,000,000	191	Canada	($48,500,000,000)
13	Malaysia	$34,140,000,000	192	India	($51,780,000,000)
14	Sweden	$28,740,000,000	193	France	($54,400,000,000)
15	Nigeria	$21,850,000,000	194	United Kingdom	($56,190,000,000)
16	Denmark	$17,080,000,000	195	Spain	($63,650,000,000)
17	Libya	$16,160,000,000	196	Italy	($67,940,000,000)
18	Iran	$15,420,000,000	197	United States	($470,200,000,000)

This entry records a country's net trade in goods and services, plus net earnings from rents, interest, profits, and dividends, and net transfer payments (such as pension funds and worker remittances) to and from the rest of the world during the period specified. These figures are calculated on an exchange rate basis, i.e., not in purchasing power parity (PPP) terms.

Source: CIA World Fact Book, 2012, https://www.cia.gov/library/publications/the-world-factbook/rankorder/2187rank.html

budget deficit must mirror each other. This was the actual case for the 1980s and into the 1990s. It led to a widespread opinion that the government deficit was *causing* the trade deficit. Then in the 1990s, the government deficit came into balance, but the trade deficit grew ever larger. The accounting identity had not changed, but the internal deficit mirroring that of trade had shifted to the household and business sectors. In the 2000s, the trade deficit was reflected by a combination of government and household deficits. The U.S. trade deficit is an exchange of foreign goods for U.S. debt. Three decades of evidence contrary to theory, however, has only been ignored, or worse, cited as evidence that still more trade liberalization is in order.

All nations which have become economic powers have protected their industries in infancy from foreign competition. This includes the United States throughout the 19th Century. The U.S. liberally employed tariffs for the protection of home-grown business and industry well into the 20th Century. Tariffs, in fact, accounted for the overwhelming bulk of federal revenues for much of this time. Likewise, Japan, China, South Korea and every other major industrial nation began with such targeted protections. Globalization denotes a regime free of such protections, but more significantly, free of obstruction to foreign ownership of domestic business and free of controls on capital flows. This is notwithstanding the fact that most successful emerging economies have relied on such controls. Figure 9-1 shows the eighteen most successful export powers in the left column. Japan, China, Malaysia, South Korea are relatively new economic powers. All depended on protections and controls as they were growing. The others newcomers are by and large oil exporters.

It is here we rejoin Joseph Stiglitz and his perspective.

Washington Consensus

The open markets and free capital flows of Globalization are two ideological pillars of what has come to be known as the **Washington Consensus**. The name derives from the proximity of the headquarters of the International Monetary Fund (IMF), the World Bank and the U.S. Treasury in Washington, D.C. The Washington Consensus paradigm combines the free capital flows and open markets of Globalization with domestic economies free from the fetters of governmental interference, and even with privatization of governmental activities. The IMF, World Bank and U.S. Treasury have been the economic and financial enforcers of this radical form of free market capitalism, sometimes designated "Neoliberalism." This is a philosophy which supposes a market answer to virtually every situation. Stiglitz defined the Washington Consensus in these terms:

> **"These policies focus on minimizing the role of government, emphasizing privatization (selling off government enterprises to the private sector), trade and capital market liberalization (eliminating trade barriers and impediments to the free flow of capital), and deregulation (eliminating regulations on the conduct of business).**

> Government had a role in maintaining macro-stability, but
> the attention was on price stability rather than on output
> stability, employment, or growth. There was a large set of
> dos and don'ts: do privatize everything, from factories to
> social security; don't have the government involved in pro-
> moting particular industries; do strengthen property rights;
> don't be corrupt. Minimizing government meant lowering
> taxes — but keeping budgets in balance."

Where the policy program of the Washington Consensus has been applied, the results have been grim. And by reason of coercion from the IMF and World Bank, it has become the applied economic regime in a great many developing countries. In East Asia, those countries like India, China, Malaysia and Vietnam which resisted free capital flows have prospered. Those which have been persuaded by the IMF and World Bank to allow capital in and out unhindered have been burned. "Hot money," capital moving in and out of markets looking for microscopic advantages, leads directly to instability.[2] A recent example of the effects of free capital flows and hot money occurred in 1997. A run on the Thai currency, the *baht*, led to what at the time was called the Asian Currency Melt-down, affecting the open economies of South and Southeast Asia. Central banks of the affected nations exhausted their reserves in a futile effort to protect their currencies. Foreign lenders panicked. Loans were called in. Massive bankruptcies ensued. The banking system went into crisis. The IMF rode to the rescue... of the foreign lenders. A laundry list of conditions was offered the affected nations in exchange for loans to effectively shift debt from the individual companies to their governments. The stipulated conditions for these loans were familiar from the Washington Consensus — government spending cuts, tax increases, and privati-zation of public services. These are called "Structural Adjustment Policies," with the ironic acronym SAP's.

Russia. Even more excruciating has been the experience of Russia since the fall of Communism. During the 1990s, in the first years of the new market economies of the former Soviet Union, the IMF and U.S. Treasury counseled free market shock therapy — immediate privatization, opening of capital markets and elimination of price controls. The result was instant economic trauma — hyper-inflation, rampant looting by government officials, takeover of the formerly state-

---

[2] Attempts to slow down this hot money has been vigorously resisted by the Washington Consensus. One good solution is the Tobin Tax, a tiny transactions tax that would be invisible to most economic actors, but would be multiplied by the number of speculative trades, thus discouraging that speculation.

owned industries by the well positioned or ruthless (the so-called oligarchs), capital flight and abandonment of a social contract with millions of citizens. The prosperity predicted by the Washington Consensus appeared in Russia, as elsewhere, in the form of Depression. Output fell by one-third from the already spare level of the Communist era. Pensioners whose stipends were fixed were wiped out by the inflation and left to sell apples in the streets or to starve. (Life expectancy itself in Russia fell by four years between 1990 and 2000.) This experience was replicated by other members of the former Soviet Union and eluded only by the few who eluded the therapy, Slovenia and Poland, for example. (Russia has recovered to its current state by virtue of oil and gas resources.)

Africa. In Africa after freedom from Colonialism in the 1960s many nations experienced a sequence of economic mistakes and misrule which brought as part and parcel large debt. The debt resulted sometimes from arms purchases, sometimes from inappropriate industrial or public works projects, often from simple graft. As a condition for financial assistance to deal with this debt, the IMF and World Bank's template demanded SAP's — the familiar strict budgetary and borrowing constraints and austerity policies. SAP's were completely inappropriate to nascent economies whose ill-educated work forces and primitive infrastructure made them poor competitors for the oft-cited but rarely seen private investment capital. Population pressures, AIDS, declining agricultural productivity and in some cases continued misrule have left desperate human conditions across the continent.

Latin America, which as Stiglitz says, "*embraced the Washington Consensus policies more wholeheartedly than any other region*" has suffered in measure. Previous to 1980, the region nurtured development by protecting its domestic industry with high tariffs. This strategy of import substitution was pioneered by the Western industrial democracies and was used extensively in the Asian success stories (although with more subtlety and government assistance).

The high interest rate policies of the United States in 1980, employed by Fed chair Paul Volcker to combat inflation, infected loans in Latin America. Debt service ballooned and triggered the default of several of the largest economies, among them Mexico, Brazil, and Argentina. In an attempt to stanch inflation and find a way out of the depression resulting from the debt crisis, Latin America embraced the minimalist government and strict austerity of the Washington Consensus. Early success soon wilted. Self-congratulation at the World Bank and IMF and commendations from their free market apologists faded. The decade of the 1980s in Latin America was lost to the debt crisis and its mismanagement. The 1990s offered only pallid growth. The **North American Free Trade Agreement** (NAFTA), another open market trade agreement effected in 1994, has proven no more fertile, and led instead to an immigration crisis.

This pattern was repeated in the aftermath of the Great Financial Crisis, even in the developed countries of Europe, where the IMF as the source of emergency capital gained a dominant voice in policy discussions. Its remedies of austerity and contraction of the public sector in Greece, Ireland, Portugal and other nations have inevitably led to economic decline and further need for emergency measures.

The Successes

The Asian success stories are China, India, South Korea, Japan, Malaysia, Singapore. These are the countries which have avoided the minimalist, market-knows-best, free capital movement approach. The governments of these nations have directed development, protected infant industries with tariffs, and ensured widespread sharing of prosperity and liberal access to education. In an earlier time, Japan was also a success story. The original postwar successes were Europe, and of course, the United States of America. All of these employed policies very unlike those imposed by the Washington Consensus.

The Marshall Plan - A Success

Just as when the New Dealers applied Keynesian programs out of political imperative, the most successful development and trade plan in history rose out of political imperative. The New Deal addressed the human needs of the Depression, but was also an answer to the domestic rise of Fascism and Communism, two competitor economic schemes which seemed to be working when market capitalism was not. As John Kenneth Galbraith said, "*The Keynesian Revolution occurred at the moment in history when other change had made it indispensable.*"

The postwar era began with American economic dominance, but Communism was alive and present in every country of Europe. (The Social Democratic parties in Europe today are, in fact, direct descendants of a non-revolutionary Marxism.) . The industrial plant of Europe and Japan had been destroyed, and that of Russia was struggling under a nascent arms race. European production facilities and farms had been decimated. Entire populations were hungry and jobless. The American answer was the Marshall Plan, named for its organizer, twice *TIME*'s Man of the Year, the "Great Man" as Truman called him, General George C. Marshall.

The Marshall Plan rebuilt Europe through billions of dollars in grants. It was a practical plan aligned with Keynes' thinking at Bretton Woods. Although the economy and infrastructure of Europe lay in shambles, an educated and skilled work force remained. Local planners and the indigenous leaders of hundreds of European communities organized the rebuilding and European labor executed it. This meant employment for the unemployed and a society reorganized around peaceful economic enterprises. It also meant immense good will toward Americans and dynamic new markets for American goods.

While the view of the American public was decidedly more open in the early 1950s than in the protectionist 1930s, fear of a return to Depression was still alive. In order to implement the Marshall Plan, the Truman Administration had to overcome resistance from many, led by Republicans, who believed the operation to be more than the nation could afford. The Keynesian demand side economics validated by the war and widely respected by the population was decisive.

Because of the resurrection of Europe as a trading partner and market for American goods, the Marshall Plan was a great source of prosperity in subsequent decades, too, perhaps surpassed only by the GI Bill in terms of practical economic benefit.

We could contrast the Marshall Plan with the largely disastrous efforts of rebuilding Iraq and Afghanistan. In these two instances, the United States chose to organize rebuilding through American contractors. It is widely acknowledged that the contractors and their several subcontractors benefitted highly, but the communities expecting new or rebuilt facilities were largely disappointed. More grievous than the corruption and inadequacy or inappropriateness of the product, perhaps, was the opportunity lost to rebuild the fabric of a country's economy by employing its domestic business and labor in productive enterprise.

Today the prosperity of Northern Europe and Scandinavia is high. The standard of living for most approaches or exceeds that of the U.S. Did Europe employ the free market fundamentalism advocated by the Washington Consensus? Was its tack to let development be organized by the vagaries of free market winds rather than by conscious planning? Quite the contrary. Government has been intimately involved with every part of these economies. Taxes have been significantly higher than even in the United States, primarily for purposes of funding social and health benefits. Public construction of infrastructure and operation of industry is common. Until relatively recently, only the United Kingdom beginning with the Thatcher era had employed a minimalist government scheme.

Because of its postwar dominance, the trade balance of the United States was invariably in surplus between the end of the war and the mid-1970s, as American manufactures, equipment and agricultural products remade the world. The industrial plants of Europe and Japan were rebuilt, but the products of their new industry were generally inferior. Fiat, meant "*Fix it again, Tony.*" Japanese-made meant cheap and undependable. Even with the oil supply shocks and price spikes during the 1970s, the U.S. maintained its trade surplus.

It is no accident that the inflection point from balance to grossly negative in U.S. trade began with the presidency of Ronald Reagan. The loose fiscal policies of the new regime in the White House were countered by tight money policies from the Fed. The dollar was made dear by restricting its supply.

A note: One effect of corporate control of the economy that John Kenneth Galbraith noted was the multiplying of the private purchasable goods at the expense of public goods. This consumer economy meant more cars, refrigerators and men's deodorant, balanced by less infrastructure, lower education and fewer social services. The focus on private goods, retail items, tradable goods, was just the mark for Japanese (and later Korean and Chinese) factories. The 1980s marked the onset, as is so often repeated here, of enormous trade deficits, the decline of American manufacturing, the explosion of public and private debt, and the experience of Globalization.

The cost of Globalization has been lost jobs and lost income. The benefit has been lower prices. Given that trade is conducted on terms so favorable to America and includes the indulgence of foreign lenders, there is little opposition to the costs. In the developing world, however, the costs of Globalization have been far worse. Two particular issues are raised here, by way of example: the need for debt cancellation and the immigration problem.

Debt Cancellation

As we have seen, many nations of the underdeveloped world were coerced into adopting Washington Consensus policies by the IMF in order to deal with the existence of huge debts. While the financial existence of this debt is confirmed by the international banks, its moral and economic existence is on less substantial ground.

Much of this debt is patently illegitimate. Much of the rest is odious. "Illegitimate debt" includes that generated by failed projects, many of which were not intended to succeed, whose primary purpose was often to use the country's treasury for the benefit of external consultants and multinational developers of large infrastructure projects. "Odious debt" is that which was contracted primarily to obtain means to oppress the population or to enrich governmental officials. Creditors are very often conspirators in all these activities, but have not been asked to share the responsibility for the consequent debt.

A further increase in the debt burden of these countries has occurred without further borrowing (or spending in the economy). This was accomplished by the capitalization of interest. A 1996 report by the British humanitarian organization Oxfam accused the World Bank and IMF of creating a "*bizarre financial circus in which more and more aid was being recycled in the form of debt repayment while the debt stock was increasing.*" The extent of this mushrooming problem is not known because of opaque reporting by the World Bank, IMF and other international lending banks.

Debt and development can be incurred on behalf of the people and for public purposes, needless to say, and need not be manipulable for the benefit of lenders, private industries, or corrupt officials. The Marshall Plan model indicates development is best organized, directed and implemented by indigenous business and labor leaders. Development on this model not only creates a facility or service more in line with domestic needs, but it creates and develops the institutions and relationships that must exist as a skeleton for further homegrown development.

There do exist examples of debt cancellation, but only in flawed forms, since they are accompanied by the stipulations of the SAP's for privatizing, budget constricting and exposing domestic markets to exploitation by multinational corporations. From the Demand Side, these are as crippling as the debt itself, and only perpetuate exploitation. Some nations spend three times or more on debt service than they spend on education.

NAFTA and Immigration

The immigration problem is popularly seen as a border security or a social fairness issue. But it is not for cherished dreams of becoming fast food counter clerks or lawn maintenance laborers that people are drawn to making the dangerous crossing into the United States. It is, rather, economic privation that drives them out of their native countries. Those who stay behind are often supported by the money sent back home from those who leave (so-called "remittances").[3]

In the U.S. Labor knows NAFTA as the vehicle that moved manufacturing jobs offshore. In Mexico, they know NAFTA as the end of the farm economy. The United States demanded under NAFTA an end to subsidies for corn and beans in Mexico. At the same time, price subsidies to the industrial farms of the U.S. were

---

[3] Many suggest that illegal immigration was actually encouraged for the purpose of generating downward pressure on wages. Virtually all agree that Globalization will have the effect of averaging out wages for unskilled workers across the planet. Both, of course, mean big losses for unskilled Americans. Immigration pressure has stopped, but it might actually be reversed if a rational farm policy at home were in place and trade and development assistance that encouraged rather than punished agrarian economies abroad were the standard. In theory everybody can be made better off from trade. In order for that to happen, however, the gains have to be distributed to everybody. When corporations control the transactions, no distribution is made, the gains are captured by the corporate sponsor.

expanded. The result was a massive dumping of cheap corn into Mexico, reducing prices by 70 percent since 1994. Farm incomes plummeted and farm families were left with a choice of crossing the border or starving. Whole villages have become ghost towns.

In the US about two percent of the population makes a living on the farm. In Mexico it is over forty percent. The Great Financial Crisis and subsequent Great Recession struck Hispanic households hardest among all U.S. ethnic groups. A Pew Research study found that two-thirds of household wealth among U.S. Hispanics disappeared as a result of the slump vs. only 16 percent among whites and 53 percent among blacks.[4] (Kochar, 2011) The conclusion must be that the U.S. militarized its borders to support an agricultural regime primarily run for the benefit of large corporate farms.

Free Trade Going Forward

The trade regime that allowed the imbalance in favor of the U.S. and developed economies was negotiated in the 1990s, with the promise that the following round of trade talks would redress these problems and benefit the agricultural economies of the developing world. The developed world — led by the United States — reneged on this promise, and the so-called Doha Round of trade talks collapsed. The farm subsidies in the U.S. and the Common Agricultural Program in Europe (which in 2011 represented 48 percent of the European Union's budget) provide the industrial farmers of the developed world a tremendous advantage over the less mechanized and less chemically dependent farmers of the undeveloped world. These interests were too powerful. New trade pacts are exclusively bi-lateral.

The Washington Consensus and rosy claims for Globalization are easily discredited, both theoretically and by the tragic empirical evidence. Where it has been tried, it has not worked. The decline following the free market shock therapy in Russia, the conditions for and failures following the Asian currency meltdown, the suffocation of Latin American and African farmers, all followed from Washington Consensus ideology. It is interesting to see social and political difficulties that accompany the attempt to apply this paradigm to the nations of Europe as a result of the debt and banking crisis there. We will look at that more closely in Chapter 12 with Nouriel Roubini.

---

[4] Simultaneously, illegal immigration from Mexico declined to zero, primarily because prospects at home became more attractive. Since the farm subsidies that advantage U.S. crops are skewed to the top. U.S. price supports do not go to the family farmer, let us be clear. Eighty-five percent goes to the largest operators.

The expansion of the U.S. following the Second World War, the resurrection of Europe and Japan, and the more recent successes in China, India, Singapore, Malaysia, and elsewhere all arose from strategies that rejected the free-market nostrums. The Washington Consensus thrived not by virtue of intellectual consistency or from ratification by results on the ground, but undoubtedly because it supports the interests of the corporate oligarchy. The free market regime of the Washington Consensus has not worked because it cannot work. Meanwhile the opportunities latent in the underdeveloped world that could be released by Demand Side schemes are foregone. These opportunities include big new markets for American goods, just as followed from the Marshall Plan. At a minimum, it is an alternative to the impoverishment and dependency of nations.

Joseph Stiglitz has much more to say to us on a much wider variety of topics, including the penetrating analysis of *Freefall*, but we will leave him here to turn to financial markets from the perspective of a man who successfully exploited them.

Chapter 10:

George Soros and the Way Markets Work

Predictions and explanations are symmetrical and reversible.

Karl Popper

George Soros is a billionaire investor and philanthropist who began professionally as an arbitrage trader in the 1960s. He developed a view of ever-expanding bubbles based on his theory of reflexivity, the two-way relationship between markets and the fundamentals they are supposed to represent. Even as he made his billions in open financial markets, Soros was notable for his philanthropic work and in supporting a broad-based 'open society' and advocating structure and government control in financial markets quite counter to the corporate control regime.

In 1992 Soros took a very large position against the British pound. When the Bank of England subsequently devalued it, the move netted him more than a billion dollars in profit. From that time forward, he was "The man who broke the pound." Others in our selection of Demand Side economists may have been asked, *"If you're so smart, why aren't you rich?"* Soros was to be asked, *"If you're so concerned with social welfare, Mr. Soros, Why did you do such a thing?"* Converted to an assertive statement, it might be, *"It's all right to profit if you're greedy, but not if you have concern for others."*

Soros' books include: ***The New Paradigm for Financial Markets, The Bubble of American Supremacy, Open Society, Underwriting Democracy,*** and ***The Alchemy of Finance.***

Demand Side sees economics as a historical science, and Soros began ***The New Paradigm*** by directly challenging the status of economics as a natural science:

"In natural phenomena there is a causal chain that
links one set of facts directly with the next. In human affairs
... there is a two-way connection between the facts and
opinions prevailing at any moment in time: on the one hand
participants seek to understand the situation (which
includes both facts and opinions); on the other, they seek to
influence the situation (which again includes both facts and
opinions). The interplay between the cognitive and manipulative functions intrudes into the causal chain so that the
chain does not lead directly from one set of facts to the next,
but reflects and affects the participants' views. Since those
views do not correspond to the facts, they introduce an element of uncertainty into the course of events that is absent
from natural phenomena."[1]

(Soros, 2008)

Demand Side analysis rejects the notion of independent variables in
economics. All variables in economics are dependent upon each other, and indeed
can morph into each other. In the late 1970s and early 1980s, for example the
money supply was restricted by Paul Volcker, then head of the Federal Reserve, as
a means of bringing down inflation. Restricting the quantity of money did not
cause prices to fall painlessly, but caused interest rates to rise and the turnover
(velocity) of money to increase. Higher interest rates meant higher costs and actually exacerbated inflation in some quarters. It also precipitated innovations, such
as the credit card.

In a thermodynamic, closed system, one could imagine the reduction of
the stock of money to have the effect the Fed imagined. Equal quantity of goods,
smaller quantity of money. Since price is the amount of money per good, prices
should fall. Or one could imagine higher interest rates discouraging spending in
some smooth and expected manner. With uncertainty, however, actors may
anticipate and rush to the entrance or exit. Economic activity may flow to sectors
perceived to be advantaged by policy.

---

[1] This echoes other Demand Side economists. For example, Robert Skidelsky, the
most famous biographer of John Maynard Keynes, pointed out that if economics were a
natural science it likely would have responded to the mathematical tools employed so
enthusiastically on its behalf to produce some significant progress. Unlike physics or
biology, and in spite of a century of effort, it has not. Skidelsky notes we are having the
same arguments today as were had in the 1930s, down to the identical level of vitriol
between the parties. (Skidelsky, 2009)

In another, simpler example, growth may lead to inflation, as companies seeing higher demand begin to invest to meet that demand and bid up the price of labor. Or inflation may lead to growth, as companies seeing rising prices move to produce earlier in the lower cost environment and sell later into the higher prices. In any event, economic variables like price, interest rates, employment rates and so on are aggregates with many components, not discrete entities which will act in the same way even in similar environments. If they were, as Skidelsky pointed out, mathematics would have done away with uncertainty, and the economic landscape would be far different than it is.

Add to this the observable fact that economics is not a closed system, and you are left with a science which resists easy translation to the regression-based models so beloved by economists. There is no fulcrum and no lever to move the models that describe the hypothetical worlds of mathematical economics. There is no causal chain that leads very far from being simply descriptive of its assumptions. Soros came to an early recognition of this in his years at the London School of Economics. Economists needed assumptions to translate their theory into *"universally valid generalizations that were comparable to those of Isaac Newton in physics."* As evidence or logic forced the abandonment of one assumption, it was replaced with another until:

> **"The assumptions became increasingly convoluted and gave rise to an imaginary world that reflected only some aspects of reality, but not others. That was the world of mathematical models describing a putative market equilibrium. I was more interested in the real world than in mathematical models, and that is what led me to develop the concept of reflexivity.**
>
>   . . .
>
> **"I contend that rational expectations theory totally misinterprets how financial markets operate. Although rational expectations theory is no longer taken seriously outside academic circles, the idea that financial markets are self-correcting and tend toward equilibrium remains the prevailing paradigm on which the various synthetic instruments and valuation models which have come to play such a dominant role in financial markets are based. I contend that the prevailing paradigm is false and urgently needs to be replaced.**
>
> **"The fact is that participants cannot base their decisions on knowledge. The two-way, reflexive connection**

between the cognitive and manipulative functions intro-
duces an element of uncertainty or indeterminacy into both
functions. That applies both to market participants and to
the financial authorities who are in charge of macroeconomic policy and are supposed to supervise and regulate
markets. The members of both groups act on the basis of an
imperfect understanding of the situation in which they participate. The element of uncertainty inherent in the two-way
reflexive connection ... cannot be eliminated, but our understanding, and our ability to cope with the situation, would be
greatly improved if we recognized this fact."

(Soros, 2008)

Soros' framework brings forward the problem of understanding the world
in which we exist by way of concepts that are necessarily symbols or shortcuts for
the purpose of reducing the mass of phenomena to a manipulable scale. The exercise leaves the investigator relating to something that is really his own
projection.

Graduating from the London School of Economics with grades too poor to
gain him entry into academia, Soros took a position as an arbitrage trader in the
United States. His interest in reflexivity and fallibility equipped him to handle the
states of nonequilibrium, boom and bust, well enough to make one fortune after
another. And indeed, markets proved to be the perfect application of reflexivity, as
market players create boom and bust by their participation, not their compre-
hension. Perception created reality, a reality that folded back on non-market
participants in often harmful ways.

Thinking about thinking, and conceptual frameworks which try to define
concepts, are inherently subject to confusion and contradiction. So when Soros
assumes an objective aspect of reality, it may become more useful, but less accurate, just as his theory predicts. Everyday events are predictable and reflexive
processes are not, he says. But it would seem that reflexivity can provide momentum in stability as well as instability.

Reflexivity

Market prices always distort the underlying fundamentals. Far from
playing a purely passive role in reflecting an underlying reality, financial markets
actively alter the so-called fundamentals. The degree of distortion may vary
widely, but the fact of distortion is not in question. This view is directly at odds

with the efficient market hypothesis and Rational Expectations theory, which maintain exactly the opposite view, that market prices accurately reflect all the available information.

Both debt leverage and equity leverage are primary pathways. Feedback loops may give the impression that markets are often right. But according to Soros, the mechanism at work is very different from the one usually imagined. That is, the connection between market prices and fundamental measurements is brought about not when markets see clearly, that is, when they assimilate information and adjust appropriately, but when they force fundamentals into line with their vision.

Reflexive feedback loops can be negative or positive. Negative feedback is self-correcting and sets up a tendency toward equilibrium. Positive feedback is self-reinforcing and produces dynamic disequilibrium. Positive feedback loops can generate wide swings, big moves, both in market prices **and** the underlying economic measurements. If it runs its full course, a positive feedback process is initially self-reinforcing upward, but when it reaches a peak, it becomes self-reinforcing downward. Soros cautions that *"positive feedback processes do not necessarily run their full course; they may be aborted at any time by negative feedback."*

Every bubble has two components, according to Soros: (1) an underlying trend that prevails in reality, and (2) a misconception relating to that trend.

> **"A boom-bust process is set in motion when a trend and a misconception positively reinforce each other.**
>
> ...
>
> **"Bubbles that conform to this pattern go through distinct stages: inception, a period of acceleration interrupted and reinforced by successful tests, a twilight period, and the reversal point or climax, followed by acceleration on the downside culminating in a financial crisis."**

(Soros, 2009)

If the trend is strong enough to survive the test of negative feedback along the way, both the trend and the misconception will be reinforced until the disconnect between the market's expectations and reality becomes undeniable. A twilight period ensues. The market continues to dance until the music stops. When the trend is reversed, the market's reflexive processes are reinforcing downward. There is no plateau other than the twilight period.

Soros originally proposed his theory in 1987 using the illustration of the conglomerate boom of the late 1960s. The underlying trend was found in earnings per share in that episode. Stock prices appreciated when earnings per share appreciated. Conglomerates learned to improve their earnings per share by acquiring other companies. Stock prices rose, allowing more acquisitions, and the process repeated. Eventually reality could not keep up with expectations. After a twilight period the price trend was reversed. All the hitherto ignored problems came to the surface, and earnings collapsed.

Typically, Soros says, bubbles have an asymmetric shape.

> **"The boom is long and drawn out: slow to start, it accelerates gradually until it flattens out during the twilight period. The bust is short and steep because it is reinforced by the forced liquidation of unsound positions. Disillusionment turns into panic, reaching its climax in a financial crisis."**

A real estate boom is a simple case. The trend of cheaper and more easily available credit combines with the misconception that the value of the collateral is independent of the availability of credit. In fact, the relationship between the availability of credit and the value of the collateral is reflexive. When credit becomes cheaper and more easily available, real estate values rise, accompanied by fewer defaults and improved credit performance. This leads to relaxation of lending standards. At the height of the boom, credit is at its maximum. A reversal precipitates forced liquidation, restricted credit, and the downward feedback loop. This is the Ponzi financing of Minsky and the debt deflation of Irving Fisher and financial Keynesians. Indeed, Soros' conclusions are quite resonant with Keynes and Minsky, although he is operating entirely within the casino market.

The international banking crisis of 1982 involved sovereign debt with no collateral. Debt ratios, like debt-to-GDP or debt-service-to-exports, were used to measure the creditworthiness of a nation, when they were actually reflexive functions of each other. The recycling of petrodollars in the 1970s increased credit flows. Debt ratios improved, stimulating even more credit, a boom. And a bust.

The Internet bubble of the late 1990s was an equity bubble. Tellingly, Soros recalls, Alan Greenspan missed the mark with his statement about *"irrational exuberance"* in 1996.

> **"When I see a bubble forming, I rush in to buy, adding fuel to the fire. That is not irrational... A well-informed and rational market can generate bubbles. And that is why we need regulators to counteract the market when a bubble is threatening to grow too big, because we cannot rely on**

market participants, however well informed and rational they are."

(Soros, 2009)

Bubbles are only the most dramatic way in which reflexivity manifests itself, and the most directly opposed to the efficient market hypothesis. But reflexivity can take many other forms. In currency markets, freely floating exchange rates tend to move in large, multi-year waves. The upside and downside are symmetrical so that there is no sign of an asymmetry between boom and bust. But there is no sign of equilibrium either.

The most critical manifestation of reflexive interaction, according to Soros, takes place between the financial authorities and financial markets. This is triggered because markets do not tend toward equilibrium. The result of periodic crises tends to be regulatory reforms, the negative feedback loop. *"Both the financial authorities and market participants act on the basis of imperfect understanding, and that makes the interaction between them reflexive."* The result is the current practice of central banking and the state of regulations.

Rational Expectations theory is incoherent on its face, Soros points out, because each market participant needs to anticipate the decisions of other market participants and know decisions before they are made. Rational Expectations theorists sought to avoid confronting this impossibility by postulating a single correct set of expectations and the convergence of people's views around it.

"That postulate has no resemblance to reality, but it is the basis of financial economics as it is currently taught in universities. In practice, participants are obliged to make their decisions in conditions of uncertainty. Their decisions are bound to be tentative and biased. That is the generic cause of price distortions."

Most often negative feedback corrects price distortions before they set in motion a boom-bust process. Market fluctuations then have a random character. These fluctuations characterize conditions near equilibrium. Far-from equilibrium situations are where a bubble predominates. Near equilibrium is characterized by routine repetitive events which lend themselves to statistical generalizations and rules that can guide decisions. It is not easy to tell how near or far one is from equilibrium. The Great Financial Crisis was a case in point.

"[There was a breakdown of] all the risk management tools and synthetic financial products that were based

on the assumption that price deviations from a putative equilibrium occur in a random fashion.... People who relied on mathematical models which had served them well in near-equilibrium conditions got badly hurt... As a participant I had to act under immense time pressure. I got the general direction of the markets right, but I did not allow for the volatility. As a consequence, I took on positions that were too big to withstand the swings caused by volatility, and several times I was forced to reduce my positions at the wrong time in order to limit my risk. I would have done better if I had taken smaller positions and stuck with them. I learned the hard way that the range of uncertainty is also uncertain and at times it can become practically infinite."

Uncertainty and its expression in volatility, that is, in wide and erratic swings in prices, cause a flight from risk, to what Keynes calls increased liquidity preference. Cash or near cash, "liquid assets," are preferred. Illiquid assets like real estate, plant and equipment are avoided. In between are companies which own the illiquid assets, but whose stocks and bonds trade on open exchanges. When a crisis abates, the liquidity preference stops rising and eventually falls in company with an almost automatic rebound in stock prices.

Soros explained the Great Financial Crisis with the following hypothesis:

"The puncturing of the subprime bubble in 2007 set off the explosion of a super-bubble, much as an ordinary bomb sets off a nuclear explosion. The housing bubble in the United States was the most common kind, distinguished only by the widespread use of collateralized debt obligations and other synthetic instruments."

The ever-increasing use of credit and leverage inflated the super-bubble. This was Soros' trend. The prevailing misconception he identified as *"the belief that financial markets are self correcting and should be left to their own devices."*

Market fundamentalism had become the dominant creed in the 1980s with Ronald Reagan as president in the U.S. and Margaret Thatcher as prime minister in the United Kingdom. The belief that markets could be left to their own devices was contradicted by a series of financial crises, but without changing the misconception. These crises included the international banking crisis of 1982, the portfolio insurance debacle in 1987, the savings and loan crisis in various chapters between 1989 and 1994, the Asian currency meltdown of 1997-98, and the dot.com bust of 2000. The financial policy makers in the Fed and Administration clung to the misconception.

> **"The authorities intervened, merged away or otherwise took care of the failing financial institutions and applied monetary and fiscal stimuli to protect the economy... These measures actually *reinforced* the prevailing trend of ever increasing credit and leverage, but as long as they worked, they also reinforced the prevailing misconception that markets can be safely left to their own devices... These crises served as successful tests of a false belief, and as such, they inflated the super-bubble even further.**
>
> ...
>
> **"The collapse of the subprime mortgage market led to the collapse of one market after another in quick succession because they were all interconnected, the fire-walls having been removed by deregulation. That is what distinguished this financial crisis from all those that preceded it. Those were successful tests that reinforced the process; the subprime crisis of 2007 constituted the turning point. The collapse then reached its climax with the bankruptcy of Lehman Brothers, which precipitated the large-scale intervention of the financial authorities."**
>
> (Soros, 2009)

That was delivered in a lecture in 2009. Was he right on this point? Or was the intervention in this most mammoth financial crisis simply the biggest successful test? At this writing the belief, or misconception, that markets can safely be left to their own devices is resurgent, and although arguments in Congress over federal government debt are contentious, the much more significant private debt bubble has not been defused. Meanwhile the Federal Reserve sponsors zero interest rates and supports to banks, as well as implicit and explicit guarantees to private credit markets to encourage more debt.

During the crisis, *"financial markets had to be put on artificial life support, extraordinary measures which eventually brought about a semblance of stability."* After the crisis, *"the episode felt like a bad dream to financial markets, which moved as quickly as possible to put it behind them and return to business as usual."*

Federal Reserve Oversight

By Federal Reserve practice the interest rate does double duty relative to the Fed's dual mandate of price stability and full employment.[2] The Fed raises the interest rate if inflation gets too high and lowers it if the economy begins to drag. In this is the implicit assumption that inflation and economic activity are two sides of the same coin (an assumption which does not bear up under scrutiny).

Under Alan Greenspan the interest rate became the Fed's only tool. When the dot.com crash was followed by the bursting of the housing bubble and then the Great Financial Crisis of 2008, the Fed's apologists argued that the Fed had no tools to contain the crisis. Greenspan argued and many of his colleagues agreed that financial bubbles were difficult to identify. It was better to clean up the mess afterward than to attempt proactive treatment. Subsequently, Greenspan adopted the position that short-term interest rates should affect only short-term investment decisions, and long-term rates like those for mortgages ought not to be laid at his doorstep. (Greenspan, 2010)

A summary from an appearance by Greenspan and his successor Ben Bernanke appearing in **The Economist**:

> **"Both men make three broad points. First, they deny that monetary policy in the early 2000s was excessively loose by traditional central-bank rules of thumb. That is a criticism frequently made by John Taylor of Stanford University, author of the Taylor rule on how interest rates should change in response to movements in inflation and GDP. Mr. Bernanke points out that based on contemporary forecasts for its preferred inflation measure, the Fed actually followed the Taylor rule reasonably closely.**
>
> **"Second, both men say there is no evidence that low short-term rates drove house prices upward. Mr. Greenspan argues that the statistical relationship between house prices and long-term rates is much stronger than with the Fed's policy rates, and that during the early 2000s the traditionally high correlation between policy rates and long-term rates fell apart. Mr. Bernanke points to structural models which show that only a modest part of the house-price boom can be pinned on monetary policy.**
>
> **"Both are equally skeptical that the increase in ad-**

---

[2] The dual mandate was established in the **Full Employment and Balanced Growth Act of 1978**.

justable-rate mortgages made short-term rates a more potent driver of house prices. Mr. Greenspan says that the pace of adjustable-rate mortgage originations peaked two years before house prices, suggesting they were not driving the bubble. Mr. Bernanke argues that the monthly payments on adjustable-rate mortgages were, on average, only 16% lower than those for fixed-rate mortgages—too small a gap to suggest that short-term rates propelled the boom.

"Third, Messrs Bernanke and Greenspan point to the global nature of the house-price boom as proof that monetary policy was not to blame. Both cite new research from economists at the Fed showing that the looseness of monetary policy in different countries was not correlated with changes in house prices.

(Economist, 2010)

Soros rejects all these claims.

"First and foremost, since markets are bubble-prone, the financial authorities have to accept responsibility for preventing bubbles from growing too big…. The authorities have, and least since the 1987 appointment of Alan Greenspan, expressly refused to accept that responsibility. Beyond this, in order to control asset bubbles it is not enough to control the money supply; you must also control the availability of credit."

Tools the Fed and other authorities had refused to use included:

- Margin requirements to reduce the use of leverage in stock speculation.

- Minimum capital requirements to prevent banks from over-extending credit.

- Explicit direction by the central bank to commercial banks to restrict activity.[3]

- A freeze on new share issuance in equity booms.

---

[3] Soros saw these explicit instructions used successfully in the 1960s and 1970s to good effect, and he noted, *"The Chinese authorities do it today, and they have much better control over their banking system."*

- Close monitoring of the positions of major market participants.

- Regulation, restriction, or prohibition of derivatives like credit default swaps.

- Regulation of synthetic securities in line with the regulation of ordinary securities.

That none of this was done, according to Soros, was "*because that would have been a violation of the market fundamentalist beliefs of Fed Chairman Alan Greenspan who could find only the money supply as a tool.*"

Perhaps most dangerous of all is the "too big to fail" guarantee, which implicitly insures the largest financial institutions. This guarantee ought never be used, opines Soros, thus those banks whom it covers

> **"... must operate on sounder footing than those banks subject to the discipline of potential failure. They must use less leverage and accept restrictions on how they invest the depositors' money. Deposits should not be used to finance proprietary trading. The compensation packages of proprietary traders must be regulated in order to ensure that risks and rewards are properly aligned. If proprietary traders are pushed out of banks into hedge funds, so much the better."**

> (Soros, 2009)

Let us return for a moment to the defense by Greenspan and Bernanke of their policy choices during the early 2000s. They contend that the easy money of that era, 1% rates for an extended period, did not stimulate the housing bubble and subsequent bust, nor with it, the explosion of Soros' superbubble.

First, it should be understood that the interest rate which the Fed and its chairmen adjusted was the federal funds rate, a very short-term rate set by the Fed, When they say that these short rates should not be held accountable for the longer-term rates, they are saying the transmission from short- to long-term is not in play. This is at odds with standard explanations. In introductory texts, long-term rates are described as derived from short-term rates with the addition of a premium to account for expected inflation.

Second, it is clear that the Fed under Greenspan purposely kept rates low to stimulate economic activity, although it may be that the chairman did not expect that activity to come exclusively in the form of a housing bubble. Today Ben Bernanke is noted for his aggressive use of so-called Quantitative Easing, which is an explicit attempt to bring down long-term rates. (This is a divergence from the practice of using the federal funds rate as the exclusive tool, but comes only after that rate has been reduced to zero and can no longer be manipulated to stimulate credit expansion.)

Finally, it is well documented that Greenspan, and virtually everyone at the Fed, took credit for the economic situation in the early 2000s, for the Great Moderation, and for the unprecedented stability they saw. They welcomed accolades and rejected criticism. To now deny responsibility is, at a minimum, counter to their previous attitudes.

If the Great Financial Crisis is to be only another test of a misconception, it will be largely through the offices of the Federal Reserve. Current chairman Bernanke's supply side credentials were validated when he became George W. Bush's chief economist in 2005. But it was his academic work on the Great Depression that earned him the appointment to succeed Mr. Greenspan. Bernanke's hypothesis is that it was the Federal Reserve of the 1920s and 1930s which caused and continued the crisis, and by extension that by saving the profligate banks rather than restructuring them, and by expanding the money supply the Depression could have been averted. Bernanke's faith in this hypothesis and his efforts to keep credit expansion for the private sector going in spite of the collapse have been heroic. Alan Greenspan was chosen for his Libertarian anti-regulatory biases by Ronald Reagan. Bernanke was likely chosen for his bias toward supporting and backstopping the banking sector.

We look again at this in the next chapter with Steve Keen, in the context of money, credit and debt.

Chapter 11:

Steve Keen and the Great Recession

> *The main constraint facing capitalist economies is not supply, but demand.*
>
> **Steve Keen**

Not surprisingly, the economist who drew the most direct line to the Great Financial Crisis was a disciple of Hyman Minsky. An Australian, Steve Keen originally trained in mathematics and came to the discipline of economics late, but with a background free from many of the distorting assumptions inculcated into students in a traditional economics curriculum, at least in the latter part of the 20th Century. He took on concepts as sacred as supply and demand curves and the "indifference curves" that underpin them. He pulled back the curtain on the 20-20 foresight assumed in the definition of "rational" in the models of the Rational Expectationist school. His training in mathematics had made him conversant with the major advances in that discipline after World War II. Those advances had bypassed the insular world of econometrics, an idiosyncratic version of mathematics taught only in economics departments. Keen's book **Debunking Economics: The Naked Emperor of the Social Sciences** examined each of the building blocks of the orthodoxy and exposed its flaws, many of which were fatal to the frameworks that had been built on them. (Keen, 2001, 2012)

Keen also took advantage of the most advanced computerized dynamic modeling software and produced remarkably accurate predictions from assumptions derived and developed from Minsky. The general equilibrium model of most forecasters, even after decades of development, produces little more than noise.

But it is his efforts in analyzing the actual workings of money and debt, and advancing accurate forecasts based on his insights, that earns him a place in this volume. In 2010, Keen won the Revere Prize,[1] given to the economist who most accurately predicted the advent of the Great Financial Crisis. In winning, Keen polled well ahead of more well-known names like Nouriel Roubini, Dean Baker, Joseph Stiglitz, Robert Shiller, Paul Krugman, Michael Hudson, and George Soros. Aside from Krugman, no Neoclassical economist received significant support in the contest, despite the dominance of this view in the field of economics.

There are reasons for this, according to Keen:

(1) Neoclassical economists — including those who run the nation's central bank and Treasury — do not understand how money is created,

(2) Orthodox economics depends on equilibrium models when the economy is never in equilibrium, and

(3) Finance, banking and debt are invisible or ignored in the models used by the mainstream to predict outcomes in an economy dominated by finance, banking and debt.

We will take each of these in order, but we note (as Keen does) the similarity of the economics of today with that which prompted John Maynard Keynes to write in 1936:

> **"Although the doctrine itself has remained un-questioned by orthodox economists up to a late date, its signal failure for purposes of scientific prediction has greatly impaired, in the course of time, the prestige of its practitioners. For professional economists, after Malthus, were apparently unmoved by the lack of correspondence between the results of their theory and the facts of observation, a discrepancy which the ordinary man has not failed to observe, with the result of his growing unwillingness to accord to economists that measure of respect which he gives to other groups of scientists whose theoretical results are confirmed by observation when they are applied to the facts."**

(Keynes, 1936)

---

[1] A prize developed by *The Real World Economics Review.* Winners were selected by a vote of their colleagues.

Endogenous Money

The orthodox understanding of how money is created has no greater advocate than Ben Bernanke, chairman of the Federal Reserve, the nation's central bank. Bernanke's academic reputation rests on his analysis of the causes of the Great Depression, as we noted in the last chapter. His efforts to increase liquidity and expand the money supply have been heroic. Results have not been commensurate with effort.

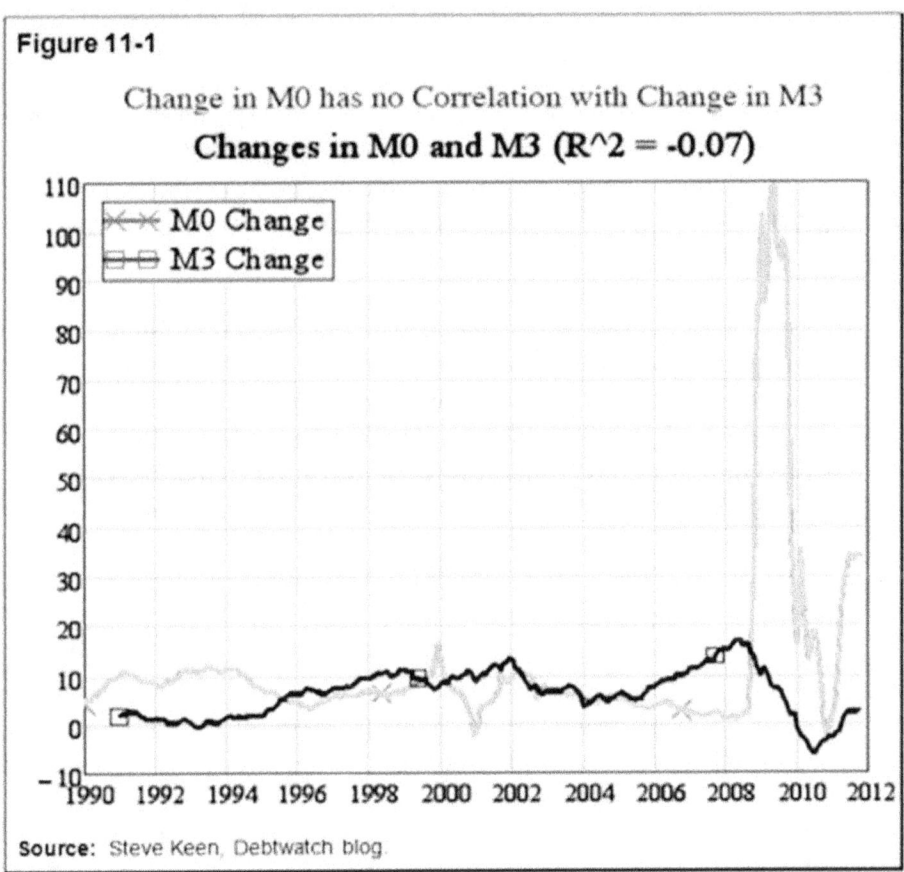

Figure 11-1

Change in M0 has no Correlation with Change in M3

Changes in M0 and M3 ($R^2 = -0.07$)

Source: Steve Keen, Debtwatch blog

The basic understanding of Bernanke and the orthodox school is that money is created by the central bank and passively expanded through the fractional reserve banking sector. *Fractional reserve* means banks hold only a fraction, say ten percent, of their deposits in reserve, and lend the rest. If the central bank increases those reserves by a certain amount, the notion is that lending and hence the money supply will increase by ten times that amount. So in response to the

Great Financial Crisis, the Bernanke-led Fed increased reserves. At the same time, the Treasury under George W. Bush recapitalized the banks through the Targeted Asset Relief Program (TARP). In Figure 11-1, the light line is the increase in reserves; the dark line is the increase in broad money.

Plainly the relationship is not what is hoped for by the Fed. Nor is it that feared by inflation hawks, who expect any increase in money to translate imme-diately and directly to prices. Rather than looking for the reasons for this discrepancy, the orthodoxy assumes the pressures are simply latent in the system, delayed for some unaddressed reason, and the debate between them is not *"Why doesn't it work?"* but, *"When will the inflation arise that is certain to follow such printing of money?"*

Money is not created passively by the banking system in this "money multiplier" manner, but actively in the banking system by the making of loans. The very act of making a loan creates deposits — money. This is by no means a new observation with Keen, and he is fond of citing the 1969 statement of a senior vice president of the New York Federal Reserve, Alan Holmes:

> **"In the real world, banks extend credit, creating de-posits in the process, and look for the reserves later. The question then becomes one of whether and how the Federal Reserve will accommodate the demand for reserves. In the very short run, the Federal Reserve has little or no choice about accommodating that demand; over time, its influence can obviously be felt."**
>
> (Holmes, 1969)

Thus, as we noted in our chapter with Hyman Minsky, booms can finance themselves by way of the banking sector. This is creation within —endogenous to — the system. It is not creation from without — exogenous — as imagined by Bernanke and the great majority of Neoclassical economists. As we will see in a moment, this misunderstanding of money goes hand in hand with a mis-understanding of debt. But first, to a more arcane issue — equilibrium vs. disequilibrium.

Equilibrium?

Economic models of the economy are abstractions, of course, like maps. Most might be thought of as flow charts, with data or equations at each gate, at the point of each arrow. The models that have received the most attention from economists are directed at explaining and forecasting the "business cycle." Wikipedia defines the business cycle as follows:

> **"The term business cycle (or economic cycle) refers to economy-wide fluctuations in production or economic activity over several months or years. These fluctuations occur around a long-term growth trend, and typically involve shifts over time between periods of relatively rapid economic growth (an expansion or boom), and periods of relative stagnation or decline (a contraction or recession).**
>
> **"Business cycles are often measured by considering the growth rate of real gross domestic product. Despite being termed cycles, these fluctuations in economic activity do not follow a mechanical or predictable periodic pattern."**

It would be easy to get lost in the arcana of economic models and their complexity. For initial clarity, we make two distinctions: (1) between business cycle models and growth models, and (2) between bottom up general equilibrium models and top down Keynesian aggregate models. Business cycle models attempt to forecast the fluctuations in output and employment. Growth models attempt to describe the parameters that determine the growth trajectory of an economy. Keynesian aggregate models use employment levels, interest rates, and other economic aggregates for prediction. General equilibrium models use raw data from hundreds of sources to patch together a supply side prediction.

The Business Cycle

The four parts of the business cycle are: peak, recession, trough, recovery. The terms "recession" and "recovery" are familiar to the lay person, but often are taken to mean "bad times" and "good times." In the study of business cycles, they instead refer to the trend. "Recession" means that things are getting worse and "recovery" means things are getting better. Thus it is possible, and now seems common, to have unemployment rates or output levels lower in a "recovery" than they were during the period of the prior "recession." [2]

The orthodox business cycle models failed to foresee the Great Financial

---

[2] The official determiner of business cycles is the National Bureau of Economic Research and its Business Cycle Dating Committee. Their determinations have not been without criticism.

Crisis and deep recession that followed. Many were puzzled, and along with the Queen of England, asked, If this was so big, *"Why did nobody notice it?"* [3] The obvious reason is that the primary assumption in these models excludes the possibility of such events. That is, they assume an equilibrium across markets, that all the flows and equations will balance, or find "equilibrium." By this assumption alone, they exclude the possibility of major economic dislocation. Hyman Minsky pointed out that if a theory excludes the possibility of depression, it is not a theory applicable to a capitalist economy. Still, and in spite of the evidence, orthodox economics has stuck to its equilibrium models.

> **"Do these failures of standard macroeconomic models mean that they are irrelevant or at least significantly flawed? I think the answer is a qualified no. Economic models are useful only in the context for which they are designed.** *Most of the time, including during recessions, serious financial instability is not an issue. The standard models were designed for these non-crisis periods, and they have proven quite useful in that context.* **Notably, they were part of the intellectual framework that helped deliver low inflation and macroeconomic stability in most industrial countries during the two decades that began in the mid-1980s."**
>
> (Bernanke, 2010) (emphasis added)

Steve Keen responded to this statement by Ben Bernanke:

> **"I make no apology for describing this argument as specious, on at least two grounds. Firstly, this argument would only be tolerably acceptable if Neoclassical economics also had well-developed models that were suitable for periods of crisis, but it does not. Secondly, this blasé acceptance that there can be bad times sits oddly against the triumphalism that characterized Neoclassical discourse on macroeconomics prior to this crisis.**
>
> **...**
>
> **"The proposition that there can be separate models for good and bad times also implies that there is no causal link between good and bad times, which would be true if they were simply the product of exogenous shocks to the**

---

[3] Reported in *The Daily Mail*, in a comment to Professor Luis Garicano, director of research, London School of Economics, Nov. 6, 2008.

macroeconomy. This is, in fact, how most Neoclassical modelers have reacted: by retrospectively treating the crisis as being not merely to unprecedentedly large exogenous shocks, but shocks which varied in magnitude over time — while still remaining negative rather than positive."

(Keen, 2001, 2012)

Indeed, as cited by Keen, the Neoclassical view is determined:

"[The] Great Recession began in late 2007 and early 2008 with a series of adverse preference and technology shocks in roughly the same mix and of roughly the same magnitude as those that hit the United States at the onset of the previous two recessions

...

"The string of adverse preference and technology shocks continued, however, throughout 2008 and into 2009. Moreover, these shocks grew larger in magnitude, adding substantially not just to the length but also to the severity of the great recession..."

(Ireland, 2011) **also** (McKibbin, 2009)

A tremendous amount of effort has been expended in building the equilibrium models up from the lowest levels of empirical data. They may include hundreds and thousands of equations and relationships. This was seen as putting macroeconomics on a firm microeconomic base. In fact, they impose the assumption of equilibrium, which means there is no possibility of explanation except external shocks. Wikipedia puts the situation and its ramifications succinctly:

"Within mainstream economics, the debate [is] over external (exogenous) versus internal (endogenous) being the causes of the economic cycles, with the classical school (now Neoclassical) arguing for exogenous causes and the ... Keynesian school arguing for endogenous causes. These may also broadly be classed as 'supply-side' and 'demand-side' explanations: supply-side explanations may be styled, following Say's law, as arguing that 'supply creates its own demand,' while demand-side explanations argue that effective demand may fall short of supply, yielding a recession or depression.

"This debate has important policy consequences. Proponents of exogenous causes of crises such as Neoclassicals largely argue for minimal government policy or regulation (*laissez faire*), as absent these external shocks, the market functions. Proponents of endogenous causes of crises such as Keynesians largely argue for larger government policy and regulation, as absent regulation, the market will move from crisis to crisis."

The Dynamics of Debt

Perhaps most surprising to the lay person will be that the models used by orthodox economists, the equilibrium models, do not include banks and financing in their flow charts and equations to a meaningful degree. As Minsky put it:

'The abstract model of the Neoclassical synthesis cannot generate instability. When the Neoclassical synthesis is constructed, capital assets, financing arrangements that center around banks and money creation, constraints imposed by liabilities, and the problems associated with knowledge about uncertain futures are all assumed away. for economists and policy-makers to do better we have to abandon the Neoclassical synthesis."

(Minsky, 1982, p. 5)

Indeed, while the average educated layman realizes the centrality of banking and finance in the Great Financial Crisis, some of the most prominent economists leading the response to the crisis did not. No less than Olivier Blanchard, the chief economist at the International Monetary Fund since 2008, said,

'The crisis has shown that large adverse shocks can and do happen. In this crisis, they came from the financial sector, but they could come from elsewhere in the future — the effects of a pandemic on tourism and trade or the effects of a major terrorist attack on a large economic center."[4]

(Blanchard, Dell'Ariccia, & Mauro, 2010)

---

[4] Blanchard's predecessor at the IMF, Simon Johnson, had a contrary view. His book *13 Bankers* (Johnson & Kwak, 2010) expresses the centrality of the banking sector in the financial crisis.

This is the common understanding of the orthodoxy which controls and supervises the banking sector. But the problem goes deeper, to a misunderstanding of the very nature of debt. The debt-deflation dynamic developed by Irving Fisher and used by Minsky and Keen is rejected by the establishment in these terms: [5]

> **"[Fisher's debt deflation hypothesis is not taken seriously] ... because of the counterargument that debt-deflation represented no more than a redistribution from one group (debtors) to another (creditors). Absent implausibly large differences in marginal spending propensities among the groups, it was suggested, pure redistributions should have no significant macro-economic effects."**

> (Bernanke, 2000, p. 24)

This conception of an economy without finance is not restricted to the Right side of the orthodoxy, but is echoed from the Left, as here by Paul Krugman:

> **"Given both the prominence of debt in popular discussion of our current economic difficulties and the long tradition of invoking debt as a key factor in major economic contractions, one might have expected debt to be at the heart of most mainstream macroeconomic models ... Perhaps somewhat surprisingly, however, it is quite common to**

---

[5] To reprise Fisher's theory, which we looked at in chapter 8 with Hyman Minsky:

According to the debt deflation theory, a sequence of effects of the debt bubble bursting occurs:

- Debt liquidation and distress selling.
- Contraction of the money supply as bank loans are paid off.
- A fall in the level of asset prices.
- A still greater fall in the net worth of businesses, precipitating bankruptcies.
- A fall in profits.
- A reduction in output, in trade and in employment.
- Pessimism and loss of confidence.
- Hoarding of money.
- A fall in nominal interest rates and a rise in deflation adjusted interest rates.

(Fisher, 1933)

abstract altogether from this feature of the economy. Even economists trying to analyze the problems of monetary and fiscal policy at the zero lower bound — and yes, that includes the authors — have often adopted representative-agent models in which everyone is alike, and in which the shock that pushes the economy into a situation in which even a zero interest rate isn't low enough takes the form of a shift in everyone's preferences.

...

"Ignoring the foreign component, or looking at the world as a whole, the overall level of debt makes no difference to aggregate net worth — one person's liability is another person's asset."

(Krugman & Eggertsson)

This *"we owe the debt to ourselves, so it doesn't really matter"* is fatal to an understanding of the real economy, but it is not so far from the common understanding, which supposes that deposits to banks are simply lent on by them to others, from patient savers to impatient borrowers. While this is not completely false, as we saw earlier, in discussing endogenous money, banks are not simple intermediaries between savers and borrowers, but lend from their own account, creating deposits simultaneously. The reserves needed are provided after the fact. So the lender is not, then, the patient saver. Likewise, the borrower is not best characterized as the impatient consumer. Schumpeter identified this borrower as the entrepreneur, the hero of the market fundamentalists.

"[The] entrepreneur — in principle and as a rule — does need credit, in the sense of a temporary transfer to him of purchasing power, in order to produce at all, to be able to carry out his new combinations, to *become* an entrepreneur. And this purchasing power does not flow towards him automatically, as to the producer in the circular flow, by the sale of what he produced in preceding periods. If he does not happen to possess it ... he must borrow it... His becoming a debtor arises from the necessity of the case and is not something abnormal, an accidental event to be explained by particular circumstances. What he first wants is credit. Before he requires any goods, he requires purchasing power. He is the typical debtor in capitalist society."

(Schumpeter J., 1934)

Beyond this, the majority of household debt is mortgage debt, which is the household's version of investment. Installment credit used to purchase autos, appliances and other durables, might also be thought of as different than consumption, as a form of investment. It is only a short step to the generalization that consumption is derived from income, and investment is derived from borrowing and lending.

We will leave this discussion in a moment, but it is important to be clear on the relative scale of debt and its distribution.

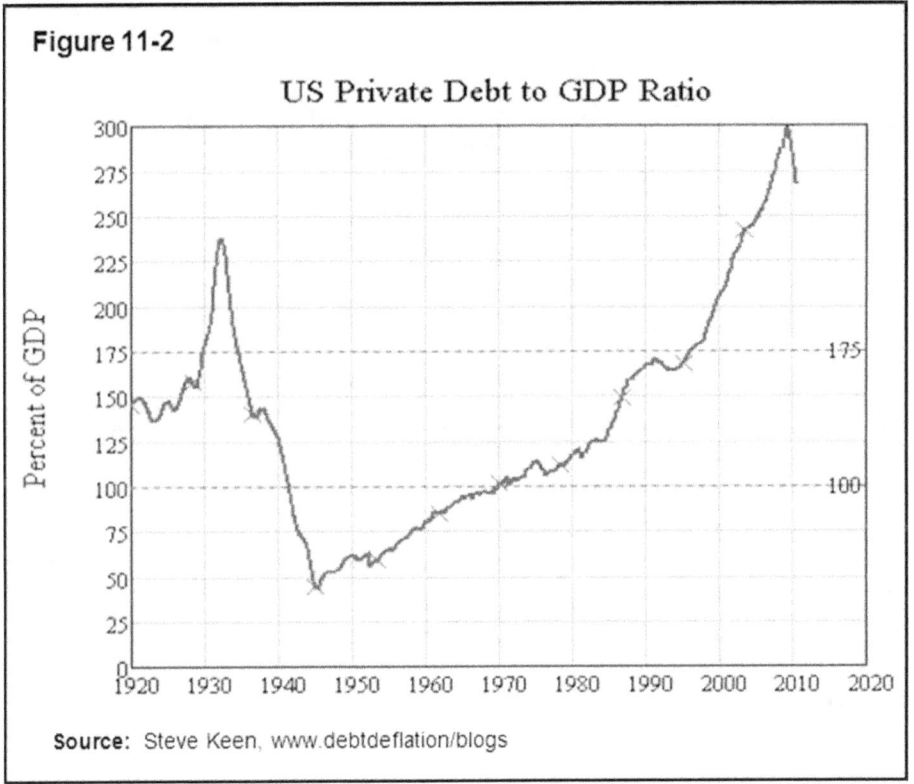

Figure 11-2

US Private Debt to GDP Ratio

Source: Steve Keen, www.debtdeflation/blogs

First, the scale of the issue. Figures 11-2 and 11-3 display the fact that the private debt in 2008 was much greater than that which ushered in the Great Depression in 1929, and that private debt dwarfs public debt. The two charts are in different formats, but it is not too difficult to see the timing as well, with the recent spike in public debt occurring after the Great Financial Crisis, while the steep rise in private debt occurred in the lead-up to the crisis.

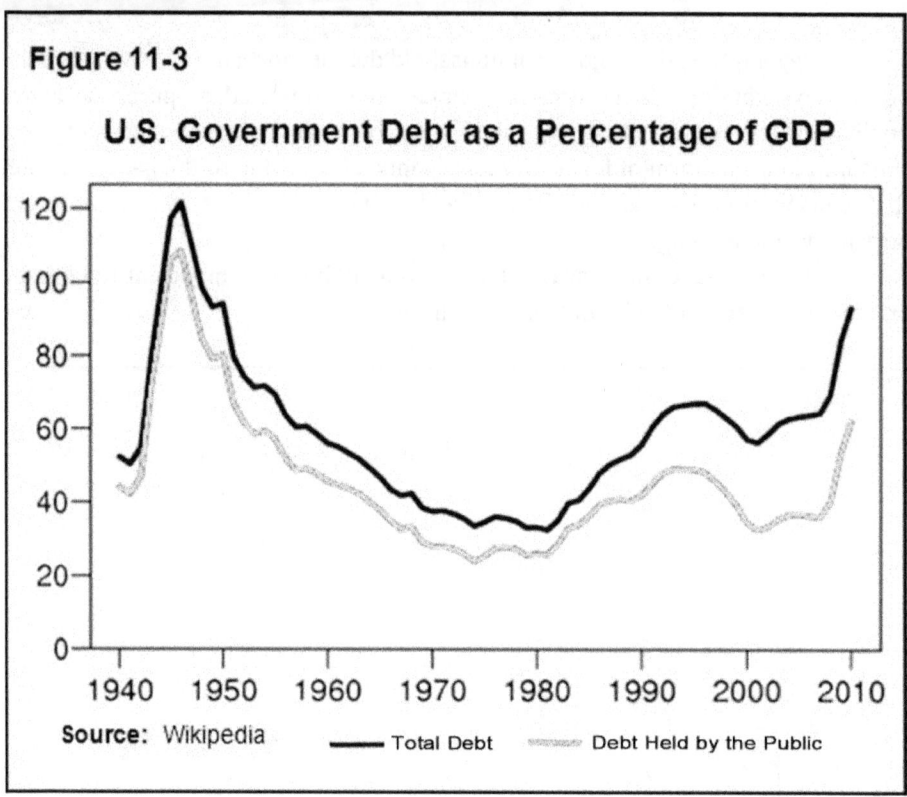

Figure 11-3

U.S. Government Debt as a Percentage of GDP

Source: Wikipedia   —— Total Debt   ∙∙∙∙∙ Debt Held by the Public

Considering that government has the additional advantages of being able to print money to satisfy its creditors and that its creditors demand only the lowest interest rates, it is not difficult to see why Minsky and Keen tend to focus on the level of debt of the private sector. We now turn to that discussion.[6]

Toward a New Macroeconomics

As Minsky demonstrated in Chapter 7, bubbles and busts are the mechanical action of the stages of financing: hedge, speculative and Ponzi. Accompanying that experience is the way money is created (or destroyed) in the modern financial economy — endogenously — not by the central bank, but within the banking system and the process of lending. It was by understanding these two

---

[6] For a description of the flows of debt and borrowing, see Richard C. Koo, "The world in balance sheet recession: causes, cure, and politics," Real World Economics Review, No. 58, December 2011, p. 19. (Koo, 2011)

dynamics, and the centrality of debt creation, and then modeling them in truly dynamic modeling, that Keen achieved a remarkable precision in what is inherently the approximate business of forecasting. (As he was doing this, the Fed with its virtually unlimited resources, produced forecasts that were fraught more often with error than insight, recalling one of John Maynard Keynes' most repeated statements: "*Better to be approximately right than precisely wrong.*")

The empirical fact that loans create deposits means that the change in the level of private debt is matched by a change in the level of money, which boosts aggregate demand. The fact that Neoclassical economists ignored the level of private debt, and actually promoted its growth, exacerbated the bubble and bust.

Keen's insight and precision in prediction stems from an appreciation of the role of debt-driven demand. ***Demand is driven by incomes and by the change in debt.*** Again, the level of incomes plus the change in the level of debt determines

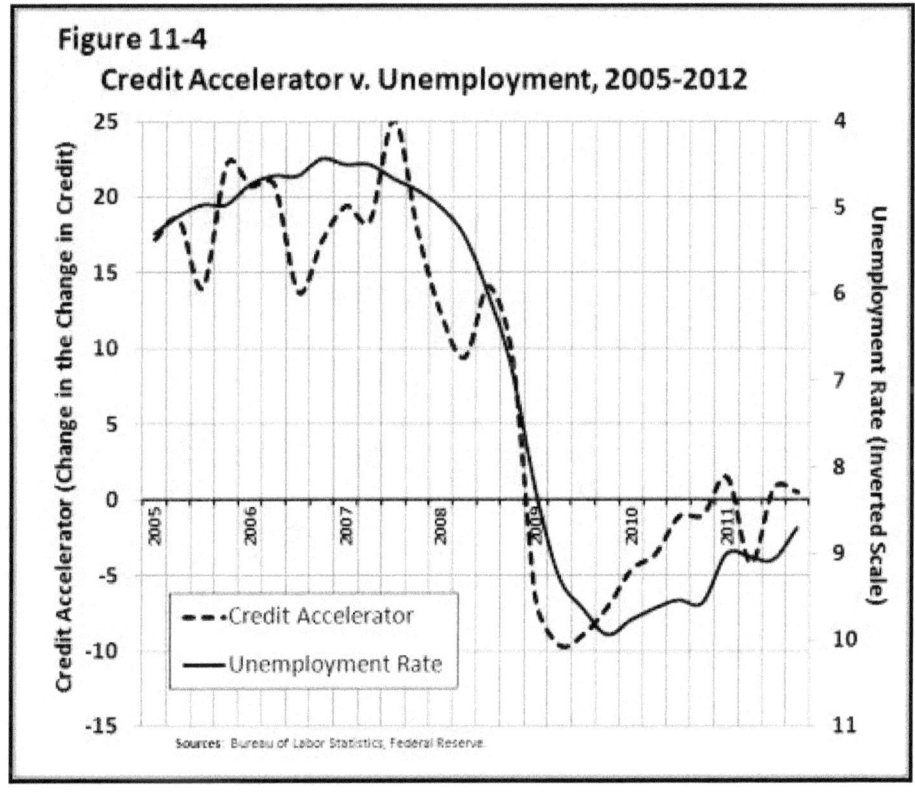

Figure 11-4

Credit Accelerator v. Unemployment, 2005-2012

Sources: Bureau of Labor Statistics, Federal Reserve.

aggregate demand. This is the key to Keen's analysis. The change in debt can be much more volatile than the change in incomes. If we think of the change in debt as the speed of the car, the change in that speed is the acceleration (which may be negative, i.e., deceleration). Keen has termed this change in the change in debt the ***"credit accelerator."***

If incomes are stagnant and net borrowing declines, then demand declines. This is what happened between the peak of the housing boom and the trough in credit. From a contribution of 12% to demand to a subtraction of 6% is an 18% swing, credit accelerator of negative 18%. This explains a great deal, including the impact on unemployment and housing, as demonstrated in Figures 11-4, 11-5 and 11-6.

Housing prices mirror the credit accelerator:

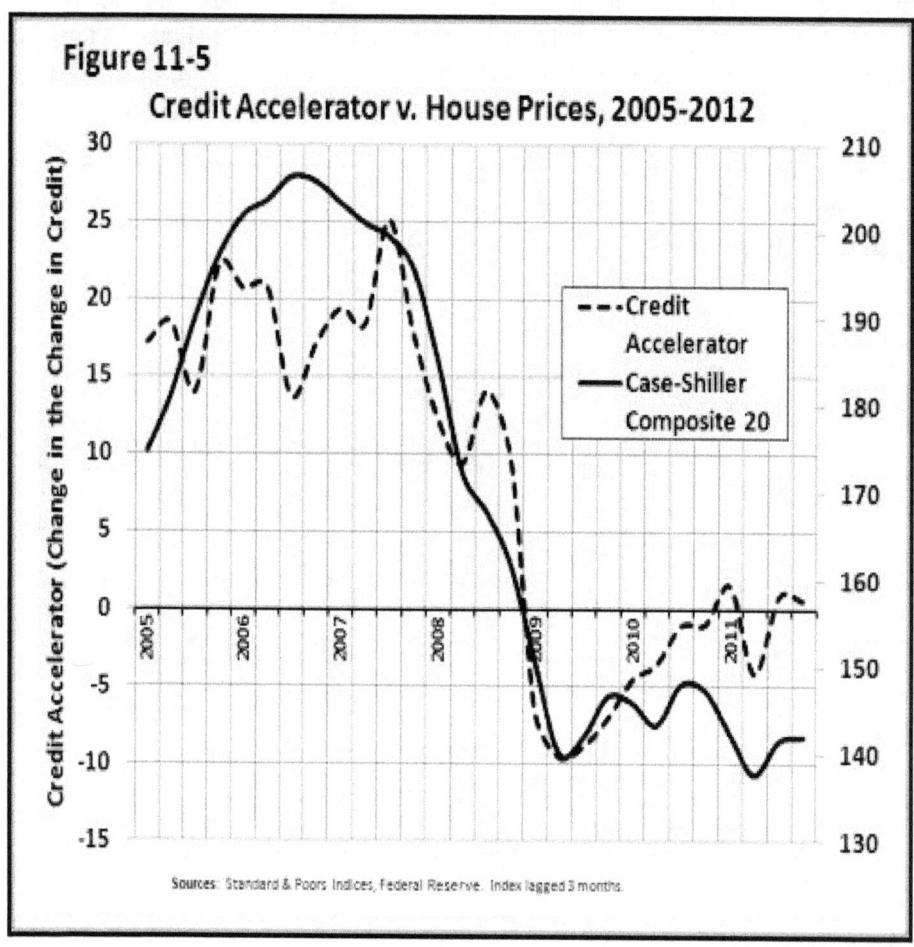

Figure 11-5

Credit Accelerator v. House Prices, 2005-2012

Sources: Standard & Poors Indices, Federal Reserve. Index lagged 3 months.

And stock markets obey as well, unless they are jinned up by extraordinary monetary policy. Both are revealed in Figure 11-6.

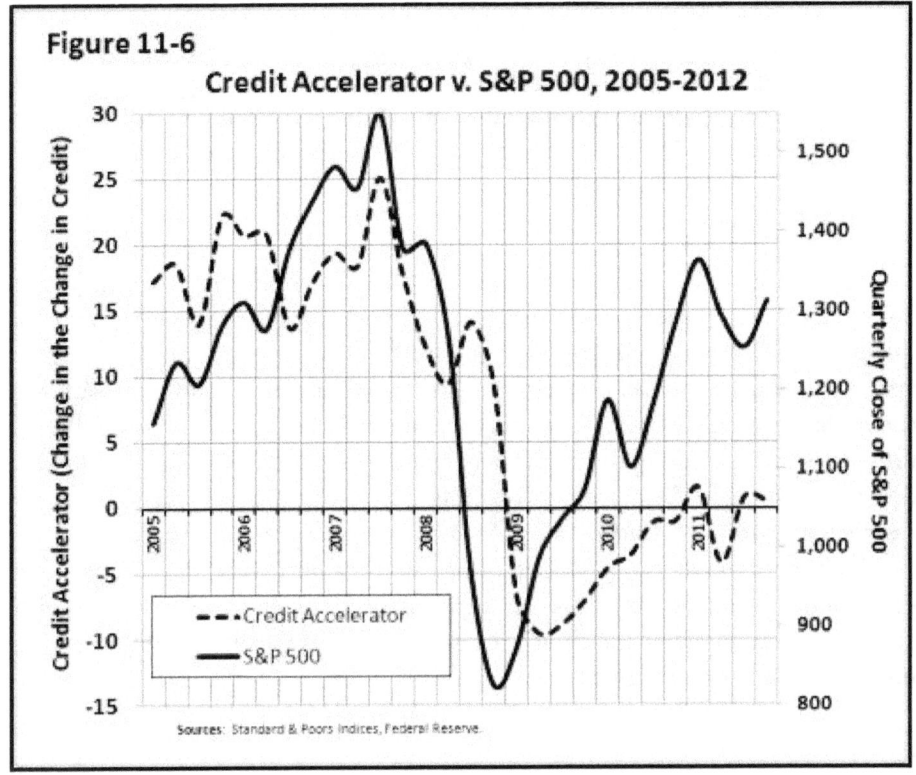

Figure 11-6

Credit Accelerator v. S&P 500, 2005-2012

So, even as the role of debt allowed Keen to predict with precision the financial debacle and economic collapse, the credit accelerator allowed him to explain the bumps and dips in the succeeding period. *"The factor that makes the recent recovery ... different to all previous ones — save the Great Depression itself — is that this strong boost from the Credit Accelerator has occurred while the change in private debt is still massively negative."* That is, even when debt is contracting, if it slows in that contraction, unemployment or other metrics may improve. This is similar to a slowing of deceleration that can be experienced as forward motion.

To put the discussion in context, we borrow (again from Keen) the description of the economic analysis that greeted Barack Obama as he entered the White House in 2009. The economic situation was precarious, but, said Edward Lazear, the chief economist for outgoing president George W. Bush, history had shown that the steeper a decline, the steeper was the subsequent recovery. The new president should be confident that strong growth, in the vicinity of five percent per year, would follow the dramatic decline.

"To give an idea of how wrong this guidance was, [Lazear's calculation] predicted that GDP growth in the two

years after the recession ended would have been over twelve
percent. If this equation had born fruit, U.S. real GDP would
be $14.37 trillion in June 2011... Instead of recovering to the
trend broken, we have recovered barely to the level of 2008
in terms of GDP, and are millions of jobs below that level in
terms of employment."

(Keen, 2011)

Debt and the change in debt also allowed Keen to identify the policy solutions that offer a realistic path to recovery. His prescription for recovery is not the
random stimulation of consumer demand proposed by many so-called Keynesians
and executed primarily via tax cuts. Nor is it the continual and futile measures by
central banks to make borrowing ever cheaper for investors. Since the core of the
problem is the debt — not the public debt, but the massive private debt — the core
of the solution should be dealing with this debt. Since the great mass of it is in
residential mortgages, a write-down of these mortgages is the starting point.

Unfortunately the mountain of private debt burdening the U.S. economy
entering the second decade of the 21st Century is beyond any level that can be efficiently serviced. A stable debt level, one which typically finances entrepreneurial
investment rather than Ponzi schemes, is about 100% of GDP. A level that will not
carry the economy downward is about 175%. As of early 2012, that private debt
level was 260% of GDP.

"The end game here will be many years in the future.
The only sure road to recovery is debt abolition — but that
will require defeating the political power of the finance sector, and ending the influence of Neoclassical economists on
economic policy. That day is still a long way off....

"From now on, unless we do the sensible thing of
abolishing debt that should never have been created in the
first place..., we are likely to be subject to wild gyrations in
the Credit Accelerator, and a general tendency for it to be
negative rather than positive."

(Keen, 2011)

Remember, the credit accelerator is operating as the general level of debt
is falling. People are deleveraging, but at a greater or lesser pace. And Soros'
reflexivity starts to work in reverse. With each plunge in asset prices, the public
becomes more wary of taking on more debt, reinforcing the downward movement.

We now turn to another man who correctly anticipated the scale and
scope of the Great Financial Crisis and whose predictions continue to prove out.

Chapter 12:

Nouriel Roubini and Crisis Economics

> *The crisis is not over; we are just at the next stage.*
> *This is where we move from a private to a public debt*
> *problem.... We socialized part of the private losses by bailing*
> *out financial institutions and providing fiscal stimulus to*
> *avoid the great recession from turning into a depression. But*
> *rising public debt is never a free lunch, eventually you have to*
> *pay for it.*
>
> **Nouriel Roubini**

Nouriel Roubini, "Doctor Doom," watched the evolution of the debt bubble from the inside. During the 1990s he was employed at the IMF and World Bank, as well as Yale University, where his emphasis was on the emerging markets and the debt crises that affected them. In 1998, he worked as an economist in the Clinton White House and then as an adviser to the undersecretary for international affairs Timothy Geithner. His book **Bailouts or Bail-Ins?** (Roubini & Setser, 2004) was devoted to the issue of dealing with bankrupt economies. *"I've been studying emerging markets for 20 years, and saw the same signs in the U.S. that I saw in them, which was that we were in a massive credit bubble,"* he said in 2009. (Bloomberg, 2009) Roubini's 2011 book, **Crisis Economics: A Crash Course in the Future of Finance** (Roubini & Mihm, 2010) laid out the analysis which informed his extremely accurate forecasts. Along with Steve Keen, Roubini most accurately gauged the broad dimensions, the range and scale, of the impending downturn.

Consonant with the views of the other Demand Side economists presented here, Roubini identified the salient features of the collapse as stagnation of incomes, a massive credit bubble and the consequent paucity of effective demand. In

"The Way Forward," (Roubini, Alpert, & Hockett, 2011) with Daniel Alpert and Robert Hockett, we read:,

> "[The] present slump is a balance-sheet Lesser Depression or Great Recession of nearly unprecedented magnitude, occasioned by our worst credit-fueled asset-price bubble and burst since the late 1920s. Hence, like the crisis that unfolded throughout the 1930s, the one we are now living through wreaks all the destruction typically wrought by a Fisher-style debt deflation."
>
> ...
>
> "[The] rise of large export-led growth economies and the growth of dollar-denominated foreign exchange accumulation set the stage for a remarkable reversal in the traditional direction of capital flows at the turn of the millennium. To be sure, capital in the form of direct foreign investment still flowed from the United States to emerging markets in order to take advantage of the massive imbalance in labor costs, but an even greater quantum of shorter term capital began to move in the other direction, much of it into the U.S. bond market, which of course exerted downward pressure on interest rates. These "reverse" net capital flows led to an excess of financial capital in the developed world — easily the most fateful result of that huge 'global savings glut' noted by then Federal Reserve Board Governor Ben Bernanke in 2005.
>
> "It was this glut which, together with the loosening of financial regulation and lending standards, provided much of the fuel to that credit and housing bubble which came to define the first decade of the 21st century. ... It is regrettable that these developments did not prompt policymakers to rethink their heavy emphasis on supply-side policies over the previous decade or two. It is equally regrettable that instead we saw a doubling down on these policies, combined with easier monetary policy and an expansion of credit meant to offset the loss of income by middle class workers. In effect, these policies amounted to a totally impractical "supply-side Keynesianism" that led to ever more borrowing meant to compensate for dwindling consumer demand no longer supported by real wages and incomes

> "These trends — global excess capacity, stagnant
> wages with rising income and wealth inequality, and global
> imbalances — all came together with a vengeance to create
> one of the largest and most destructive credit bubbles in
> world economic history."
>
> (Roubini, Alpert, & Hockett, 2011)

In a 2007 speech to a gathering of the economic and financial elite in Davos, Switzerland,[1] Roubini predicted an imminent housing collapse followed by financial disruption. This view was starkly counter to the conventional complacency that strong growth and low inflation would continue — the so-called "Goldilocks" economy: Not too hot, not too cold. That economy, Roubini suggested, was threatened by three ugly bears — a U.S. mortgage meltdown, the end of cheap credit and higher oil prices — which would seriously crimp consumer demand and usher in a recession. His view darkened after Davos, and he predicted a systemic financial crisis, not just in the U.S., but globally.

At the time, Roubini's remarks occasioned more laughter than concern. He was dismissed immediately by the assembled bankers, government officials and academic economists. The next year, after the housing market had collapsed, and the exposure of banks and other lenders conformed to the scale he had predicted, Roubini returned to Davos, no longer at the fringe, but at the head of the table.[2] But Dr. Doom's outlook had not improved.

> "2008 will be an ugly year... How bad will it be? I
> think it will be extremely severe. When you add up all the
> losses, not just subprime, but soon enough auto loans, credit
> cards, student loans, leveraged loans and corporate bonds,
> we're looking at $1 trillion of losses in the financial system....
> There is serious risk of a systemic financial crisis. Not just in
> the U.S., but globally."
>
> (Roubini N. , 2008)

At the onset of the housing meltdown a great deal of faith was put in the Fed. Part of this trust derived from the "Great Moderation," Roubini's "Goldilocks" period, which saw steady growth and moderate inflation. This was proof to the

---

[1] "Davos" is officially the "World Economic Forum." It takes place in January.

[2] That occasion heard the comments of Fed Chair Ben Bernanke, who is reported (by Joseph Stiglitz) to have said, "Nobody saw this coming," when in the first row sat Stiglitz, Roubini, Robert Shiller and others who had seen it coming and had spoken out about it. A lesson in the insular nature of the orthodoxy.

orthodoxy that a new command of the economy had arrived. Where Minsky and Keen saw these periods of stability as the incubators of instability, the Fed and its proponents found confidence and validation. In the chapter with George Soros, we saw this period was by no means free of financial crises, and these crises tended to serve not as harbingers of trouble, but as successful tests of the orthodox view. This market confidence was some-times termed the "Greenspan Put," a Wall Street reference to the willingness of the Fed to do whatever was necessary to reverse stock market slides.[3] In fact, the sole strategy and tactic of the Fed in crises in the Greenspan era, from his appointment as chair in 1987 and on into the 2008 period, was to increase liquidity, to make sure nobody with good collateral was forced to sell into a falling market and to flood the market with money. This eager-ness to provide liquidity began with the 1987 crash. Greenspan later admitted that he did not know until a late spate of buying that the action would work. (Greenspan, 2010) That buying may well have been due to leveraged purchases by speculators using the cheap Fed funding. This process of floating the stock market on easy money continues today with the Quantitative Easing programs.

We should also recall that the Great Moderation and its various financial crises occurred in the context of a great stagnation of incomes of the middle class. (See Figure 12-1.) The trajectory of incomes flattened out along with the general economy in the U.S. between the late 1970s and 2008, before beginning to fall. It is best described by median household income. Corresponding to this flattening of middle class incomes was a decline in the overall growth trend (Figure 12-2) and the expansion of the financial sector as a proportion of the economy (Figure 12-3). (That expansion was seen in the charts of indebtedness in the previous chapter.)

The financialization of the economy, the growth of public and private debt, stagnating middle class incomes and flattening growth have all followed the movement up Minsky's financing structures, from productive "hedge" financing, through rollover "speculative" financing, into bubble "Ponzi" financing. Financial markets are themselves internally driven from the Demand Side. Traditional banks make money by writing loans and collecting interest. The more debt, the more profit. If banks can increase the demand for debt, they do better. On the other side, as returns to investment decline, money flows into the riskier assets, from the stocks in the dot.com era, to housing, and into real estate and sovereign debt in peripheral European nations. The flood of money into these riskier assets drives down interest rates, but also reduces lending standards.

---

[3] A "put option" is a financial market instrument that allows one party to sell a certain stock to the second party at a certain date at an agreed upon price. Puts are bought to hedge against downside risks.

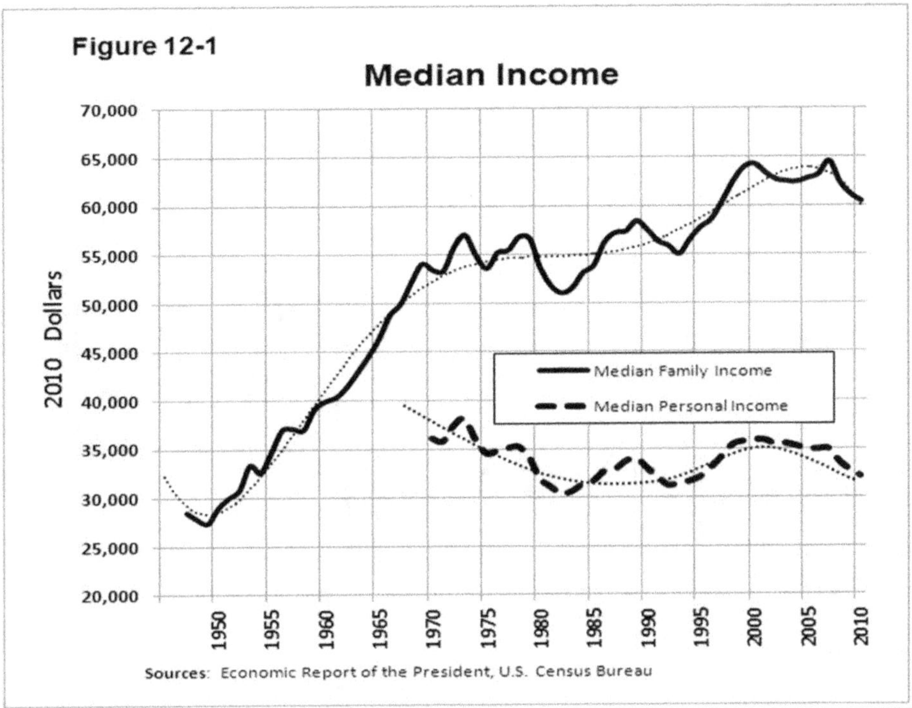
Figure 12-1
Median Income
2010 Dollars
70,000
65,000
60,000
55,000
50,000
45,000
40,000
35,000
30,000
25,000
20,000
1950
1955
1960
1965
1970
1975
1980
1985
1990
1995
2000
2005
2010
Median Family Income
Median Personal Income
Sources: Economic Report of the President, U.S. Census Bureau

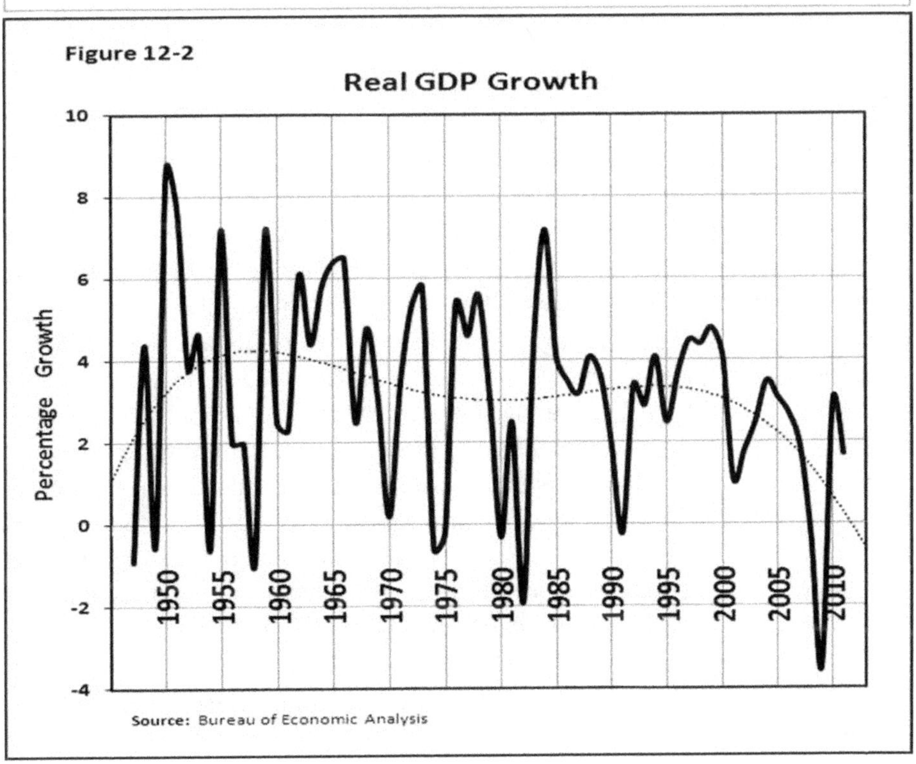
Figure 12-2
Real GDP Growth
Percentage Growth
10
8
6
4
2
0
-2
-4
1950
1955
1960
1965
1970
1975
1980
1985
1990
1995
2000
2005
2010
Source: Bureau of Economic Analysis

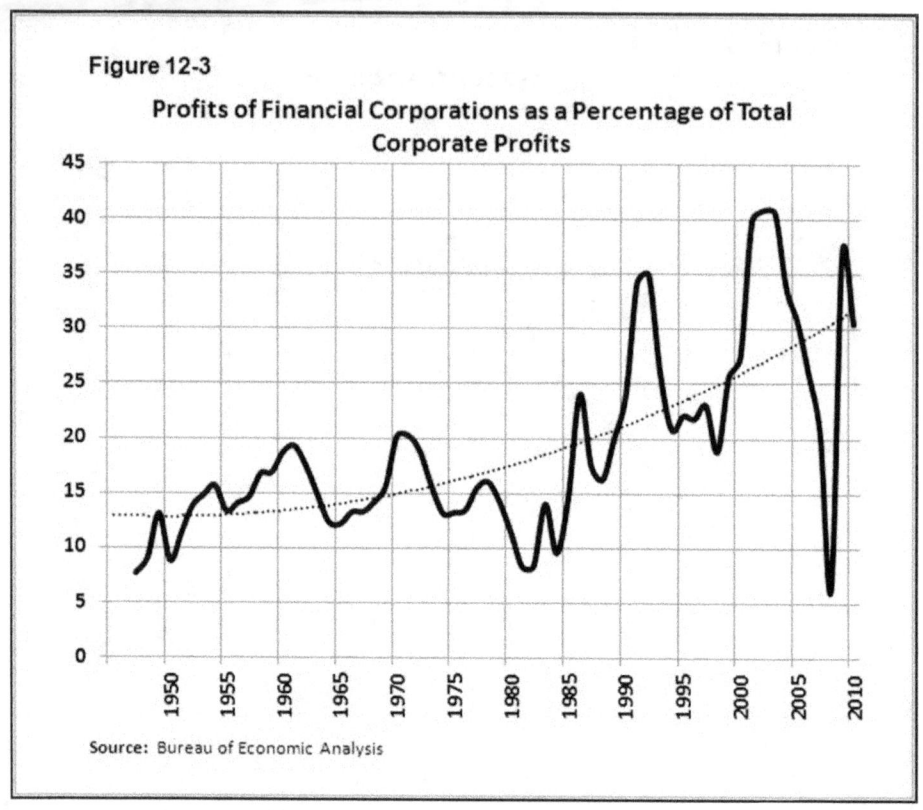

Figure 12-3

Profits of Financial Corporations as a Percentage of Total Corporate Profits

Source: Bureau of Economic Analysis

The economic position of the financial sector has risen in tandem with its political influence. In terms of James K. Galbraith's corporate oligopoly, Finance today is the captain and its lieutenants are the major corporations. So when the financial ruin forecast by Roubini at Davos materialized, it was not surprising that policy-makers rushed their taxpayers into the breach, not on behalf of the stricken homeowners or newly unemployed, but on behalf of banks and lenders. These were the powerful constituents whose interests demanded priority. Banks were recapitalized, credit markets received central bank guarantees, financial institutions and corporations saw their costs of capital reduced dramatically, secret loans were extended to hundreds of favored companies, and the Federal Reserve even bought outright $1.25 trillion in mortgage-backed securities (MBS) that had gone bad. Meanwhile tens of millions of mortgage borrowers, homeowners, watched trillions of dollars in paper wealth evaporate while the trillions of dollars in debt remained to darken their financial futures.

Government did not ignore completely the downturn in the real economy. But economic stimulus that was labeled "Keynesian" came primarily in the form of tax cuts, and only modestly in the form of public works or support to state and local governments. It was the Keynesianism of Ronald Reagan. (We will visit the dynamics of true Keynesian stimulus in the next chapter.) Even this real economy stimulus, when it did not lead to immediate and total recovery, was abandoned.

The tectonic plates had been shifting for decades during the fitful Goldilocks period. The tremors that produced the first cracks in the financial system began in April 2007 with the Federal Home Loan Mortgage Corporation (Freddie Mac) announcing it would no longer purchase the most risky mortgages or mortgage securities. Mortgage lenders began to fail, ratings agencies began downgrades of mortgage bonds, hedge funds began to suspend redemptions or fail outright, the banks began to acknowledge their own off balance sheet holdings. In December the Fed voted to cut rates, began to take mortgage-backed securities onto its balance sheet, and provided liquidity help to European banks. The onset of the recession was dated from this month — December 2007. (Although a majority of orthodox economists were still projecting the nation would avoid that recession several months later.)

In February 2008 the economic downturn prompted a $180 billion stimulus program signed by George W. Bush. (This was the first "timely, targeted and temporary" stimulus we address in the next chapter.) In March, the Fed rushed aid to the major investment and trading houses and facilitated the takeover of Bear Stearns, one of the five largest. The federal funds rate was cut to 2.25 percent. Major and minor banks exposed to mortgages and mortgage securities began to fold. Emergency support to Fannie Mae and Freddie Mac turned into conservatorship — the two giant mortgage buyers had failed.

Roubini had predicted the sequence of events as it played out, but it was only in September 2008, when another of the big five investment banks, Lehman Brothers, failed that the markets dropped their pretense and conceded that this was not a manageable financial event. A great many in the financial sector cite the failure of Lehman as the catalyst for the crisis, not just the largest event. The Financial Crisis Inquiry Commission (later convened to examine the causes of the crisis for Congress and the president) adopted a middle ground:

> **"The crisis reached seismic proportions in September 2008 with the failure of Lehman Brothers and the impending collapse of the insurance giant American International Group (AIG). Panic, fanned by a lack of transparency of the balance sheets of major financial institutions, coupled with a tangle of interconnections among institutions perceived to be 'too big to fail,' caused the credit markets to seize up. Trading ground to a halt. The stock market plummeted. The economy plunged into a deep recession.**

"The financial system ... bears little resemblance to that of our parents' generation. The changes in the past three decades alone have been remarkable. The financial markets have become increasingly globalized. Technology has transformed the efficiency, speed and complexity of financial instruments and transactions. There is a broader access to and lower costs of financing than ever before. And the financial sector itself has become a much more dominant force in our economy.

"From 1978 to 2007, the amount of debt held by the financial sector soared from $3 trillion to $36 trillion, more than doubling as a share of gross domestic product. The very nature of many Wall Street firms changed from relatively staid private partnerships to publicly traded corporations taking greater and more diverse kinds of risks. By 2005, the ten largest U.S. commercial banks held 55 percent of the industry's assets, more than double the level held in 1990. On the eve of the crisis in 2008, financial sector profits constituted 27 percent of all corporate profits in the United States, up from 15 percent in 1980. Understanding this transformation has been critical to the Commission's analysis."

The Commission concluded:

The financial crisis was avoidable

- Widespread failures in financial regulation and super-vision proved devastating to the ability of the nation's financial markets.

- Dramatic failures of corporate governance and risk management at many systemically important financial institutions were a key cause of this crisis.

(Financial Crisis Inquiry Commission, 2011)

Other conclusions specified excessive borrowing, poor government response, a breakdown in accountability and ethics, collapsing lending standards and dark market derivatives.

The central question identified by the Inquiry Commission was:

"How did it come to pass that in 2008 our nation was forced to choose between two stark and painful alternatives

— either risk the total collapse of our financial system and economy or inject trillions of taxpayer dollars into the financial system and an array of companies, as millions of Americans still lost their jobs, their savings, and their homes?"

In answering this question, the Inquiry Commission pointed to failures of people and institutions. It did not issue an opinion on whether Keen's and Soros' debt bubbles existed. It did, notably, mention Galbraith's corporate oligarchy, at least generically.

"[Regulators] lacked the political will — in a political and ideological environment that constrained it — as well as the fortitude to critically challenge the institutions and the entire system they were entrusted to oversee.

"Changes in the regulatory system occurred in many instances as financial markets evolved. But as the report will show, the financial industry itself played a key role in weakening regulatory constraints on institutions, markets, and products. It did not surprise the Commission that an industry of such wealth and power would exert pressure on policy makers and regulators. From 1999 to 2008, the financial sector expended $2.7 billion in reported federal lobbying expenses. Individuals and political action committees in the sector made more than $1 billion in campaign contributions. What troubled us was the extent to which the nation was deprived of the necessary strength and independence of the oversight necessary to safeguard financial stability."

(Financial Crisis Inquiry Commission, 2011)

A good illustration of this latter point was offered when the Commission's findings were muted, at least from a public relations standpoint, by a separate report from a dissenting minority of Republicans, sponsored by the financial sector, who attacked the government instead of banking practices. Notably the Fed as the primary regulator was absolved by this minority, who focused instead on the quasi-governmental agencies Fannie Mae and Freddie Mac.

As remarkable as the financial collapse itself, and perhaps more destructive, was the absence of reform. Nor was there substantial change to the power elite in place before the crisis. The top corporate executives who had over-

seen the crash maintained their positions in the aftermath. The political estab-
lishment changed only slightly when the Obama administration took power in
January 2008. The architects of too big to fail banks and the drafters of deregu-
lation became the insiders in the administration of Barack Obama. (These included
Robert Rubin and Lawrence Summers, Clinton-era Treasury Secretaries, and
Rubin protégé Timothy Geithner, who rose to that post under Obama.)[4]

Fraud, widespread from top to bottom was never seriously prosecuted.

In spite of the disaster unfolding and then lingering, the intellectual flexi-
bility remained among economists on Wall Street, in Academia and in the political
structure to avoid accountability for the ramifications of the financial sector
debacle. The philosophy that nurtured the crisis was the free market Washington
Consensus, yet when the U.S. and European banks and shadow banks lurched into
insolvency, they were not ruthlessly liquidated as demanded of such institutions in
other places and times. Their shareholders were not wiped and their managements were not replaced. Instead, the Washington Consensus was suspended for a
time, as banks and quasi-banks were recapitalized at government expense, and
bank cash flows are still favored by public policy. Their senior managements
continued to receive huge rewards.

The explicit premise of aborting the market discipline of failure in the big
banks was that these financial institutions were needed for recovery. *"First the
financial sector, the real economy would follow."* Within three years after the 2008
crash, corporations were achieving record profits, banks held record reserves, and
the real economy continued to languish. Bernanke's hypothesis and the trillions of
dollars that followed it into action were blithely and limberly ignored. The austerity demanded of developing economies by the Washington Consensus and its
enforcers at the IMF was deemed not appropriate for the authors of that
prescription.

The sum of direct aid to the financial sector, the one-time stimulus
programs, and the reduced revenues resulting from the deep recession were toted
up in the category of government deficits. Deficits burgeoned in most nations
worldwide. In the U.S., the deficit ran from an already high $413 billion under
George W. Bush in pre-crisis 2004 to over $1.4 trillion in 2009, and has remained
over $1 trillion.

Rather than recapitalizing the government via tax increases or assistance
from the central bank, and seeing that the corporations and major banks were

---

[4] Then-Senator Phil Gramm, the Republic politician most aligned with
deregulation and expansion of financial corporations, was the designee for Treasury
Secretary by John McCain, Obama's 2008 election opponent, until well into that campaign,
and well after the results of the big bank policy were tragically evident.

safely out of harm's way, policy simply went back to the Washington Consensus. The agenda turned smoothly from banking practices, fraud and assistance to homeowners and settled on the profligacy of government and how to reduce social insurance and onerous regulation. The Washington Consensus had returned to power. Ironically, as noted in the chapter on Minsky, government deficits actually support the cash flows of corporations and are algebraic identities to profits in the absence of real investment. Neither taxing these profits, nor reducing deficits (and profits) by cutting social insurance is likely to be deemed politically feasible.

It was the falling of dominoes identified in Roubini's 2007 analysis at Davos: Rising oil prices, the mortgage meltdown, the end of cheap credit, a systemic financial crisis that would spread globally.

Of these, we have ignored the factor of oil prices, and this is perhaps a good place to discuss them. Historically, rising oil prices have presaged economic downturns and recessions. A good study of this was done by Andrew Oswald, et al. (Oswald, Caruth, & Hooker, 1998) Oswald forecast the recession of 2000 when other economists were enchanted with the idea of a "New Economy" and the end of the business cycle. The dot.com crash in the stock markets and the tragedy of 9-11 have been cited as the impetus for the 2000 downturn. But the catalyst was undoubtedly the rising price of oil (which came off a floor of $15 per barrel that was enjoyed for much of the Clinton expansion) combined with rising interest rates. The Fed under Alan Greenspan raised interest rates to historic real highs just as oil prices rose in 1999-2000. A similar pattern triggered the 2007 slow-down with Ben Bernanke at the helm of the Fed.

From the Demand Side it is not difficult to see why oil and interest rates affect the economy. Oil is resource-based. The rise and fall in its price produces no new jobs. Insofar as higher costs reduce consumer demand for other products, oil price hikes actually reduce jobs. The same is true of interest rates, which increase costs without increasing any kind of production, and in fact, will reduce pro-duction insofar as demand for goods is reduced. This will be explored more fully in our next chapter, in the section on the multiplier.

A pattern of real economy slowdown led by oil prices and interest rates followed by a financial crisis is too marked to ignore. It is a mistake to conflate the two — a real economy downturn and financial crisis — but also a mistake to ignore the relationship.

Roubini's summary of his 2008 speech in January at Davos:

"The U.S. has already entered into a recession and this recession will be much uglier than the mild recessions of 1990-91 and 2001, as a shopped out, saving less and debt burdened consumer is on the ropes and faltering.

"The world will not decouple from the U.S. hard landing; there will be significant recoupling and a sharp global economic slowdown. When the U.S. sneezes the rest of the world catches the cold; and today the U.S. will not experience just a simple common cold but rather a protracted and severe case of pneumonia; thus, the real and financial contagion to other economies will be severe.

"Whatever the Fed does now is too little too late; the Fed had a wrong diagnosis of the economy and was behind the curve for over a year. The Fed claimed that the housing slump would bottom out a year ago; instead we have the worst housing recession in U.S. history still getting much worse now. The Fed claimed that the subprime would be a niche and contained problem; instead we have had massive contagion to the entire financial system as a credit bubble and excessive debt and leverage occurred throughout the economy and the financial system. The Fed claimed that the housing problems would not spread to the rest of the economy; instead we have had real and financial spillovers and now a fall of most components of aggregate demand: housing, capex [capital expenditure, i.e., investment] spending, commercial real estate investment and now, ominously, private consumption that represents 70% of demand.

"The U.S. stock market is now entering a seriously bearish territory and will fall much more sharply throughout the year as earnings sharply drop in the recession; the Bernanke put and the aggressive Fed easing will not rescue the stock market or the financial markets, as a severe recession is unavoidable regardless of what the Fed does. Fed easing cannot resolve severe insolvency problems among consumers, mortgage lenders, home builders, highly leveraged financial institutions and, soon enough, among over indebted corporate firms.

"Equity markets around the world are now plunging and will plunge much more as investors are realizing that a severe U.S. recession will lead to a sharp global economic slowdown and a significant fall in profits across the world. In an integrated global economy both economic growth rates and markets are highly correlated.

"Many risky assets will face downward pressure in 2008, not just U.S. and global equities: junk bond yield spreads will widen as bankruptcies spread; corporations will default in great numbers; housing bubbles will pop in many countries and lead to falls in home prices; securitized products — in housing, real estate and otherwise, will experience further massive losses.

"Losses in the financial system will be greater than $1 trillion; thus there is a serious risk of a systemic banking and financial crisis. The credit crunch will become much more severe as capital of financial institutions is eroded and reintermediation of financial flows into the banking system occurs."

(Roubini N. , 2008)

Certainly Roubini's vision was prescient. Events occurred very close to the lines he had mapped out, including the global dimensions of the problem. *"The global economy was being supported on one engine, but the U.S. consumer is shot."* But it is instructive to see here where he missed the mark.

Yes, there was a systemic banking crisis that required massive bailouts, backstopping and continues to require distorting policy.[5] Yes, housing bubbles popped in the U.S., Ireland, Spain and elsewhere, carrying down with them employment and mortgage lenders. But no, corporations did not default in great numbers. U.S. auto manufacturers went under, but were reorganized. Many other corporations weathered the storm in spite of hits to revenues by cutting workforces, refinancing at new lower rates, eliminating new investment, and relying on government to support consumer demand. Four years after the crisis, corporate profitability was at record highs.

Spreads widened enormously in some cases,[6] as Roubini suggested they would, but in other cases the spreads were contained, as investors such as pension funds reached for yield in the absence of returns from government bonds.

Although U.S. stocks crashed to half their values, they recovered nicely with the Bernanke-Greenspan put. Retail investors left stocks in great numbers and did not return, but professional investors were active, supported by Fed policy and needing returns that could no longer be found elsewhere. This was not fore-

---

[5] The Fed's zero interest rate policy is purported to be dedicated to stimulating investment, but a huge beneficiary is the banking sector, which can borrow from the Fed at zero and lend to the Treasury at higher rates, and pocket the difference.

[6] A "spread" is the difference between the interest rate of a safe government bond and that of a more risky corporate or less safe government bond.

seen at all by Roubini, who predicted stocks would weaken with the economy, only to see a surge in stock prices after mid-2008.

Also arising out of the collapse was the phenomenon of commodities as an investment class. Formerly commodities were considered the product of investment. The companies that mined or grew or otherwise produced the commodities (oil, corn, copper) were objects of investors' interest. The commodities themselves were not, and the futures markets were used to protect against price swings. As the uncertainty over the scale of the downturn rose in late 2007, and perhaps fearing inflation from Fed easy money policy, investors turned to commodities as investments themselves and to futures as bets in the casino. Banks, such as J.P. Morgan Chase and Morgan Stanley became owners of tens of millions of barrels of oil inventory, funded with the cheap credit from the Fed.. A massive commodity bubble ensued (See Figure 12-4).

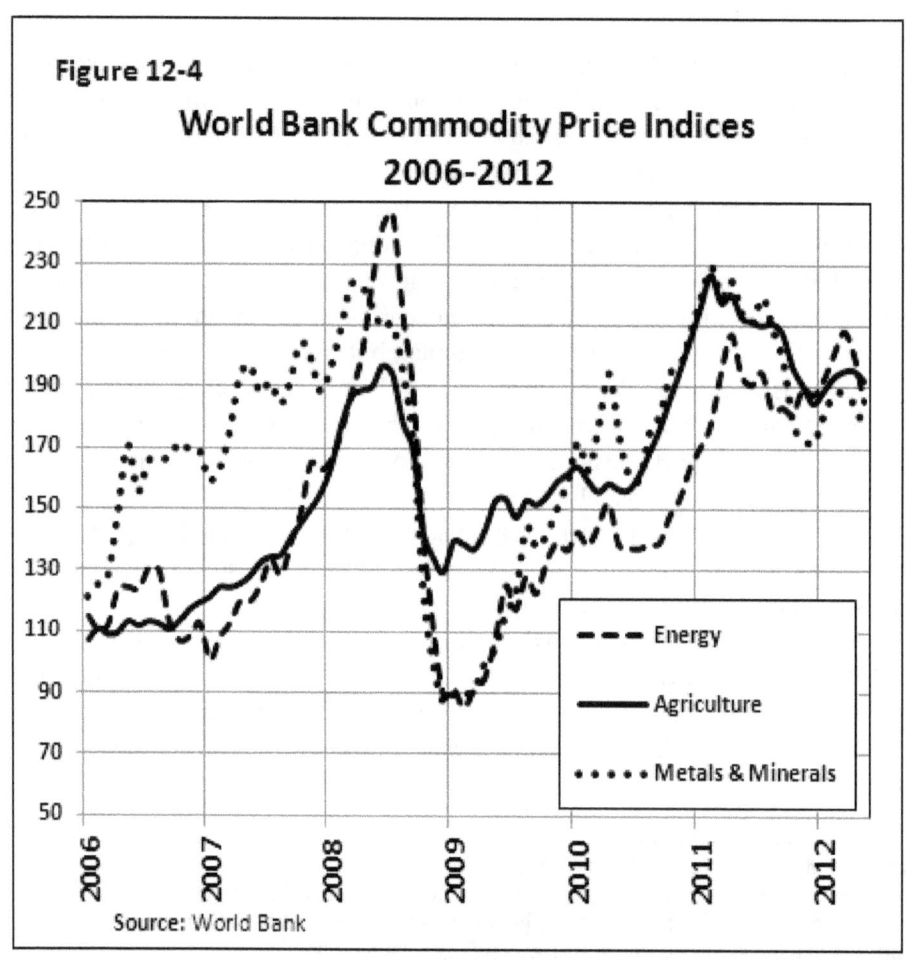

Figure 12-4

World Bank Commodity Price Indices
2006-2012

Source: World Bank

Oil prices rose dramatically to over $145 per barrel in June 2008, two and a half times the level a year earlier. Corn, wheat, copper and virtually all other commodities followed in train. A new investment vehicle, the exchange traded fund (ETF) became the means for individual and institutional investors to participate in what is essentially speculation. Commodities futures markets, previously used by commercial interests to protect against price swings, became the arena for speculation. It was estimated by one industry insider that speculation moved from 30 percent of the market for oil to 70 percent. (Guilford & Greenberger, 2012) Worldwide, the higher prices for agricultural products caused by the commodity bubble resulted in hunger and social unrest.

A typical explanation for these events was provided by the World Bank:

> **"World food prices increased dramatically in 2007 and the 1st and 2nd quarters of 2008 creating a global crisis and causing political and economic instability and social unrest in both poor and developed nations. Although the media spotlight focused on the riots that ensued in the face of high prices, the ongoing crisis of food insecurity has been years in the making. Systemic causes for the worldwide increase in food prices continue to be the subject of debate. After peaking in the second quarter of 2008 prices fell dramatically during the late-2000s recession but increased during 2009 and 2010, peaking again in early 2011 at a level slightly higher than the level reached in 2008. However a repeat of the crisis of 2008 is not anticipated due to ample stockpiles.**
>
> **Initial causes of the late-2006 price spikes included droughts in grain-producing nations and rising oil prices. Oil price increases also caused general escalations in the costs of fertilizers, food transportation, and industrial agriculture. Root causes may be the increasing use of biofuels in developed countries and an increasing demand for a more varied diet across the expanding middle-class populations of Asia.**
>
> (World Bank, 2012)

This explanation is not convincing from the demand side. If consumer demand were the source, prices should have fallen from the years of high growth and incomes. In fact, they became most volatile after the beginning of the recession. Further, commodity prices became correlated across the board, rising and falling together, which is difficult to explain with supply shocks or specific demand strength. The conclusion is almost inevitable that the behavior of these markets — the prices of commodities — is driven not by real economy events, but by financial markets, and further, that hunger deprivation and social unrest are direct and indirect outcomes of the current policy framework.

But with no change in these factors, the commodity bubble broke in mid-summer 2008, on the eve of the Lehmann Brothers debacle. By the end of 2008, oil had plummeted to just over $30 per barrel. This commodities bubble has been largely invisible to economists, as has a second, which began in early 2011 and reached a peak later that year.

ETFs and commodity derivatives have been the sources of demand for commodities and have kept prices high in the face of lagging consumer demand. These markets are suspect for being manipulated, and some charts display an un-likely regularity in their movements. The Fed provided both the fuel for this fire and the need for warmth, as its easy money was available to speculators while the cold from declining returns in other investments stimulated interest in the hot new vehicles.

In the last analysis, Roubini was right. The crunch on consumer demand of high debt, falling incomes and a suddenly dysfunctional financial system played out in a systemic failure of the banking system. Consumers were "tapped out, saving less, debt burdened." The situation was mitigated only by policy canted heavily toward corporate interests and the financial sector. The incomes from lost employment and lower returns on traditional investments were replaced to some degree by government deficits, but these incomes show no signs of recovering of themselves, or returning to pre-crisis levels.

As the crisis moved from the U.S. housing finance market to the global economy, Roubini followed it. It is to that we now turn.

The Collapse of the Eurozone

In a manner quite reminiscent of his work running up to the Great Financial Crisis, Roubini outlined the path to breakup of the European Monetary Union — commonly called the Eurozone — those nations in Europe who adopted the common currency the *euro*. It was again, at Davos, but a year earlier than his "three ugly bears."

> **"[There] is serious growth divergence in the Eurozone area. ... This growth divergence is becoming a serious threat to European Monetary Union. (EMU). As an increasing number of European observers are suggesting, different countries are coping differently to these challenges. ... Germany has reacted with corporate restructuring, cutting**

labor costs and 'competitive deflation.' ... Italy has done
little and is experiencing 'stag-deflation,' a combination of
stagnation and deflation. ... Similar competitiveness problems are faced by Greece, Portugal and Spain."

(Roubini N. , 2006)

When the recession brought on by the financial excesses in U.S. housing
reached Europe, it exposed this problem and more that Roubini outlined in 2006,
and we will return to that speech later, but first a bit of context.

In the classical sense, trade between countries should balance. If wine is
traded for wool, it will be a simple barter and the exchange will depend on who
wants what and how much they are willing to give for it. When money acts as a
medium of exchange, it simply allows barter of many goods in different quan-
tities, but the result is Country X has the goods of Country Y in exactly the same
propor-tion as would be derived by barter.

Complications arise with the introduction of money as a store of value,
debt and credit.

1. If Country X wants to export more than it wants to import, say to satisfy
   its wool exporters while protecting its domestic wine makers, it can do
   so by lending money to Country Y to buy its product. This is done
   simply by accepting the currency as payment. (The face of a dollar bill
   makes this connection explicit: *"This note is legal tender for all debts
   public and private."*) So accepting this debt is what China and Germany
   and all net exporters must do, in fact, to avoid a balanced trade in
   goods and to be "net exporters." When they convert their currency, as
   prudent money managers, into interest-bearing notes, it is not the
   profligacy of the borrowers, but the interests of the lenders at play.
   Again, the currency of the U.S. has become a *store of value*, which will
   be taken and held as a reserve against future instability. These
   "reserve currencies" are seldom held as simple stacks of banknotes or
   liquid deposits, but are typically used to purchase bonds that pay
   interest in the reserve currency country. This converts the store of
   value into the debt. (China or Germany could buy real assets — houses,
   factories, stocks of other countries, but unless they can move these to
   their own soil — which would then be "trade" — the effect is the same
   as lending.)

2. Money itself as a store of value in addition to a medium of exchange has
   history. Commodity money like gold was the common currency for
   centuries. The great wealth of Spain after 1500 came from its exploi-

tation of the gold riches in the New World — instead of printing money, they mined it. Aside from decorative purposes, gold has no real utility. In this respect, when the dollar is accepted everywhere in the world, for transactions as disparate as cab rides and ransom payments, the dollar is "as good as gold." All foreign banks hold dollars as reserves, in the same way they hold gold.

Except:

3. The exchange rates of currencies, their prices in terms of each other, may vary. The money of one country, aside from the dollar in some situations, is not widely used in other countries. Nobody in Japan wants Polish *zloty*. They don't spend as well as *yen* in Tokyo. The currencies themselves can change in relation to each other, thereby adjusting the effective prices of the goods, and thus balance trade. No longer can you get three bales of wool for three kegs of wine, now you can only get two. The price of wool has gone up in the wine-producers' country by 50 percent. Yet when currencies adjust to each other with regard to trade, those adjustments also affect all the loans denominated in those currencies. So if the dollar is not worth ten *yen* any more, but only eight, you have lost twenty percent on your loan. (In this sense, some see gold as a currency with a supposedly stable value.)

Be careful to observe that when we say "country," we are talking not about the government of that country, but about the combination of government, business and household sectors together. If the combination is running a trade deficit, the country is adding to its debt — public or private — and the effect is the same.

Growing out of the Common Market, the European Union was organized as a free trade zone for the benefit of its constituent nations, to establish the "free movement of people, goods, services and capital." A subset of EU members established a monetary union and on January 1, 1999, adopted the *euro* as their common currency and sole legal tender. Countries which are members of the European Union, but are not in the EMU and which retained their national currencies, include: Denmark, Hungary, Poland, Sweden and the United Kingdom, as well as the smaller Eastern European nations of Bulgaria, the Czech Republic, Latvia, Lithuania and Romania.

From the beginning, concern was raised over the stability of monetary union without fiscal and political union. Could nations share a common money without the ability to tax in common or move spending counter to the trade flows? Proponents of the *euro* believed it to be a step to political and fiscal union.

Opponents believed fiscal union was a necessary first step, to be implemented prior to monetary union.

One analysis of international trade, that of Nobelist Robert Mundell, suggested that trading nations could have any two of three options: a stable exchange rate, the free flow of capital, and/or domestic fiscal sovereignty. This became known as "Mundell's Trilemma," or the "Unholy Trilemma," because of course, nations would like all three. Without going into the details of the analysis, we note here that it has proven relevant in practice. Countries like Japan, the United States, Great Britain, Sweden and others, have chosen floating exchanges rather than stable, pegged rates. These countries have enjoyed the free flow of capital and domestic sovereignty. China and others have chosen to peg exchange rates, that is, to stabilize them. These nations have retained domestic policy sovereignty by controlling capital flows, not allowing easy entry into their domestic economy nor allowing money to flow freely out of the country. The members of the Eurozone chose a stable exchange rate when they agreed to the single currency. They welcomed the free flow of capital, and indeed, the attraction of many nations to the *euro* was that it reduced the costs of borrowing. Consequently, those nations are on the third horn of the trilemma, they are facing the relinquishment of fiscal sovereignty.

Unfortunately for these countries, the authority to which they have ceded sovereignty is the amorphous Market, or its disorganized surrogates in the "Troika" — composed of the European Union, the European Central Bank and the International Monetary Fund. Even more unfortunately, the preferred fiscal program of the Troika is austerity, privatization and the rest of the Washington Consensus. Economist Dani Rodrik has offered an alternative. He opined that capital will control in a "golden straightjacket" those who become dependent, and as Mundell's Trilemma indicates, this will mean ceding control of sovereignty to the financiers, but suggests that democracy can expand beyond the nation state and subsume the actions of the financial markets. (Rodrik, 2007, 2002)

Control of capital flows via a clearing union has been proposed by Paul Davidson, among others. (Davidson, 2009) This would allow governments to manage trade imbalances within a currency union, shift the onus for imbalances to the net exporters, as well as minimize tax avoidance and financing of illegal activities. A clearing union would effectively neutralize the trilemma and bring financial markets under sovereign control.

The alternative of ceding sovereignty is characterized now in Europe as accepting "fiscal union" on the heels of the monetary union which formed the *euro*. Let us look at what this, and the trilemma untamed, has meant for one country.

Greece

In one way, Greece is the special, dysfunctional case in the Eurozone. Much of its economy escapes government control and taxation, pension benefits are outsized, and corruption is widespread. In another way, Greece is the poster child of the Eurozone problem. At the beginning of the crisis, Greece held a large government debt in relation to GDP (105 percent in 2008), a significant trade deficit (which means it continued to borrow, adding to its pile of debt) and as a member of the Eurozone, an exchange rate could not be adjusted (there is no exchange rate).

Since government debt is periodically rolled over, the carrying cost of the debt is quite sensitive to the interest rate. An interest rate of 2% on government debt and a debt load of 100 percent of GDP means that two percent of GDP would be needed to service that debt. An interest rate of 15% means fifteen percent of GDP would be needed. But if the debt burden is higher than 100 percent, say 140 percent, then a 15% rate translates to twenty-five percent of GDP just to service the debt. But what happens when revenues are raised by way of taxes and are not spent in the country, but moved as debt payments to another country? As the Greeks found out, the economy shrinks. GDP is smaller, and the debt burden is greater.

Greece underwent a sequence of austerity measures of just this kind at the insistence of its foreign lenders and the European central authorities. Just as the recession born in the USA hit and the Demand Side response indicated expanding deficits, Greece was forced to attempt to contract. The government deficit rose from €14 billion to €24 billion. GDP rose only €3 billion. The government debt as a percentage of GDP rose to 142 percent. (Eurostat, 2012) At this writing the interest rate on ten-year Greek bonds is nearly 30%.

The austerity exercise persuaded the population of the madness of the prescription, but not the madness of the doctor, nor the wisdom of leaving the currency union. Popular support for remaining in the *euro* was likely driven by memories of the good times, recognition of a corruption in domestic governance, and fear of the unknown in a return to the *drachma*.[7]

---

[7] Roubini suggested restructuring the debt in 2006. Joseph Stiglitz called for solidarity between the Eurozone countries in 2008, possibly "eurobonds," essentially tying the debt of all countries together and creating a single, presumably low and serviceable, rate of interest. Interestingly, Stiglitz also pointed out that Germany's leaving the Eurozone would have produced the greatest beneficial effect, since it would have accomplished a functional adjustment in exchange rates, one which might have corresponded to trade flows. The *euro* is high for most countries, but low for Germany.

Roubini summarized the situation:

> "For the last decade, the PIIGS (Portugal, Ireland, Italy, Greece, and Spain) were the Eurozone's consumers of first and last resort, spending more than their income and running ever-larger current account deficits. Meanwhile, the Eurozone core (Germany, the Netherlands, Austria, and France) comprised the producers of first and last resort, spending below their incomes and running ever-larger current-account surpluses.
>
> "These external imbalances were also driven by the *euro*'s strength since 2002, and by the divergence in real exchange rates and competitiveness within the Eurozone."

(Roubini N. , 2011)

"Competitiveness" here refers to what has to happen in the internal domestic economy in order to rebalance trade in the absence of an exchange rate that adjusts. It does not mean that the Greeks must retool to produce Audis. Wages must be adjusted downward, meaning a new austerity, an internal deflation, as opposed to the inflationary process that would occur with the revaluation of currencies, where prices would rise for imports and for domestic goods with external markets. The relative effect is similar, but the adjustment process is more difficult. Special interests would vie for privileged exclusion from an internal deflation.

More important is the impact on debt. Debts denominated in a country's own currency fall with its exchange rate, reducing the effective debt burden. When there is no exit, and an internal deflation is the course chosen, the austerity demanded means the relative weight of the debt increases as the incomes needed to pay it are cut. The only way left to reduce debt is to write down the principle, restructure it. This is what was being attempted for Greece in a contentious multi-party negotiation in 2012.[8]

The internal contradictions of disparate economies marching to the same monetary structure cannot be resolved if the political system does not allow it. In Europe, as in the U.S., control of policy rests inordinately with the entrenched

---

[8] Notice that the U.S. is similar to the PIIGS in that it has been the consumer of first and last resort to the world. The U.S. differs because its currency is independent, and further, the dollar is accepted as a store of value. Notice, too, that the deficit of the U.S. is far higher than would be permitted as a member of the Eurozone.

economic elite. When the two largest economies, Germany and France, met to decide policy for all, each brought the needs of its banks to the table. It was the fragility of these banks, not the situation in Greece that was of paramount concern. European banks in 2011 were even less well-capitalized than their U.S. counterparts at the time of the 2008 crisis, and they are larger as a proportion of their economies. The European Central Bank (ECB) is independent of any mandate except to minimize inflation. In the negotiations which formed the currency union, control of the ECB was ceded to the Germans, and to their legacy of fear from the hyperinflation of the Weimar Republic, leading to an exaggeration of anti-inflation measures in policy.

But Greece is a small country, about two percent of the Eurozone in terms of GDP, and its contradictions or those of other smaller nations — Portugal, Ireland, Cyprus — could be contained. In 2006, Roubini pointed to the same problems in a far larger nation — Italy.

"[The] lack of serious economic reforms in Italy implies that there is a growing risk that Italy may end up like Argentina. This is not a foregone conclusion, but if Italy does not reform, an exit from EMU within five years is not totally unlikely. ... Italy faces a growing competitiveness loss given an increasingly overvalued currency and the risk of falling exports and growing current account deficit. The growth slowdown will make the public deficit and debt worse and potentially unsustainable over time. And if a devaluation cannot be used to reduce real wages, the real exchange rate overvaluation will be undone via a slow and painful process of wage and price deflation. But such deflation will keep real rates high and exacerbate the growth and fiscal crisis. Without necessary reforms, eventually this vicious circle of stag-deflation would force Italy to exit EMU, return to the *lira* and default on its *euro* debts [by way of unilaterally converting its debt from *euro* to *lira*]....

[A] sovereign nation is able to follow such policies — EMU exit, return to national currency and effective default on *euro* debt — regardless of any legal or formal constraints that the EMU treaty imposes in terms of no exit clauses. This is not science fiction, as Argentina was forced to do the same.

"What would be the systemic effect of such Italian exit from EMU? They would be extremely severe on EU capital markets as Italy would default on some of its external debt — the part of its *euro* debts held by non-residents. The contagion effects to other EU capital markets and banks would be severe. And the no bailout rule of the ECB would become effectively threatened as the ECB would be forced to monetize both liquidity and solvency induced runs to avoid a systemic effect on EU financial markets.

"In conclusion, my view is that EMU can work and has worked for the Eurozone countries that have reformed and are reforming. But, unless Italy and other Eurozone laggards change their policies to pursue serious economic reforms that restore competitiveness and growth, they will eventually be forced to exit EMU. This would be a disaster, but a disaster that may become unavoidable unless policies change. And I am currently pessimistic about the chances that such changes may occur given the policy makers and policies currently in place in countries like Italy."

(Roubini N. , 2006)

The failure to fix the financial sector after the 2008 U.S. collapse exacerbated the conditions which threatened to spread the Eurozone collapse across the globe in 2012. In 2008, derivatives such as credit default swaps and loan guarantees were traded out of sight, in "dark markets," prior to their showing up in the taxpayer-funded bailouts of American International Group (AIG) and the affected banks. Derivatives are still traded in dark markets. During the meltdown of European sovereign debt, these unregulated, invisible derivatives link banks across the world, even as the European's greater leverage ratios make those banks more vulnerable to insolvency. These derivatives are sometimes described as hedges or insurance, designed to limit risk. In practice they are simply speculative bets. There is no insurable interest necessary. Derivatives serve to increase risk, not reduce it. The restructuring or writedown of debt — which may be essential to the solvency of nations — creates the credit event that triggers the derivatives. Avoidance of these credit events is as much a concern in the deliberations over Greece and others as is the direct impact on under-capitalized banks. The failure of austerity to produce sturdy debt repayment is evidence of the fundamental error of that policy.

Roubini identified the means to an orderly escape from the Eurozone crisis: a "symmetrical reflation" policy of easy money, unlimited lending from the ECB to those sovereigns which were solvent, a depreciation of the *euro* vs. other global currencies, and economic stimulus to the core to provide demand and markets for the periphery. In the end, these options were rejected, primarily for fear of inflation. The powerful at the core insisted instead on an asymmetric adjustment.

> "The bitter medicine that Germany and the ECB want to impose on the periphery ... is recessionary deflation: fiscal austerity, structural reforms to boost productivity and reduce unit labor costs, and real depreciation via price adjustment as opposed to nominal exchange-rate adjustment.

> "The problems with this option are many. Fiscal austerity, while necessary, means a deeper recession in the short term. Even structural reform reduces output in the short run, because it requires firing workers, shutting down money-losing firms and gradually reallocating labor and capital to emerging new industries. So to prevent a spiral of ever-deepening recession, the periphery needs real depreciation to improve its external deficit. But even if prices and wages were to fall by 30% over the next few years (which would most likely be socially and politically unsustainable), the real value of debt would increase sharply, worsening the insolvency of governments and private debtors.

> "In short, the Eurozone's periphery is now subject to the paradox of thrift: increasing savings too much, too fast, leads to renewed recession and makes debts even more unsustainable. And that paradox is now affecting even the core.

>   ...

> "Of course, such a disorderly Eurozone break-up would be as severe a shock as the collapse of Lehman Brothers in 2008, if not worse. Avoiding it would compel the Eurozone's core economies to embrace the fourth and final option: bribing the periphery to remain in a low-growth uncompetitive state. This would require accepting massive losses on public and private debt, as well as enormous transfer payments that boost the periphery's income while its output stagnates.

> "Italy has done something similar for decades, with its northern regions subsidizing the poorer Mezzogiorno. But such permanent fiscal transfers are politically impossible in the Eurozone, where Germans are Germans and Greeks are

Greeks... [The] monetary union's slow-developing train wreck will accelerate as peripheral countries default and exit.

...

"With Italy too big to fail, too big to save, and now at the point of no return, the endgame for the Eurozone has begun. Sequential, coercive restructurings of debt will come first, and then exits from the monetary union that will eventually lead to the Eurozone's disintegration."

(Roubini N. , 2011)

What does this mean on the ground, in the real economy? The financial sector has once again contracted with debtors in a failed enterprise, accepting payment for the risks it took. But when the enterprise failed, it has not accepted its part of that risk. It has demanded the pound of flesh be donated entirely by the other party, or by the governments of those nations in which the parties operated. It must do this, the financial sector reasons, because its own solvency depends on it. The belief remains that individual banks, or even the group as a whole, with only more time, can weather the macro problems of under-employment and widespread idleness. So the sector has insisted on policies that lead to the inevitable contraction of economies, the self-defeating debt-deflation cycle. It is the ruin not only of the debtors, but inevitably the lenders as well. The economy can be organized to produce full employment and security, both individual and societal, but until financing and the financial sector become aligned to the needs of the real economy — instead of the reverse — crises will continue.

Chapter 13:

Next Steps from the Demand Side

> *The enemy of conventional wisdom is not ideas, but the march of events.*
>
> **John Kenneth Galbraith**

In our concluding three chapters we will expand and apply the work of our economists. In this chapter, we look at some Demand Side concepts that have not yet been explored fully. In Chapter 14 we will survey markets themselves, why they differ from the idealized fundamentalist view and how they need to change to more closely approximate the efficiency that has been claimed for them. In the final chapter, we forecast what the economic dysfunction of the current day is likely to mean, particularly in terms of the challenges of global warming, global poverty and economic stability.

The economists presented here have illustrated the primacy of demand in economics. What is demanded is what is produced. Things are not produced unless they are demanded. As Steve Keen said, **"The main constraint facing capitalist economies is not supply, but demand."** Unless suppliers are successful in meeting, or controlling, that demand, they go out of business. Corporations are extremely successful at this managing of demand — the military-industrial complex in maintaining a tremendous war machine, consumer goods giants in manufacturing need for brands, the health care industry in selling a system rather than outcomes, the oil industry in maintaining reliance on the doomed technology of fossil fuels, and so on. And our economists have identified the importance of debt and financial markets in determining economic events in the context of policy dominated by an entrenched financial sector.

But our Demand Side minds, to this point, have not left the private sector conceptually. The government exists to regulate the private sector and provide social insurance to mitigate the harsh outcomes which attend Capitalism. There are some elementary concepts that need to be added. None of these is original with the author, but neither is any allocated its full share of application by the economists presented here. We have chosen four to treat in detail:

- **Public Goods**
- **Natural Monopolies**
- **The Commons**
- **The Multiplier**

Public Goods

So far in our treatment we have imagined an economy in which capital and labor combine to produce output which is undifferentiated GDP. But products and services are divisible into two broad categories — ***public goods*** and ***private goods***. Public goods account for an immense proportion of the well-being of a society and its citizens, in part because they are useful in themselves and in part because they generate wealth to private economic actors. Public goods contrast to private goods — those material and personal benefits which obsess us, consumers and economists, and which are created and consumed in abundance. Private goods are the cars, houses, restaurant meals, magazine subscriptions, computers, trips to Hawaii, jewelry, food, and on and on. These are marked by two distinctive characteristics. Private goods are ***excludable*** and they are ***depletable***.

Excludable means that to a greater or lesser degree the use or enjoyment can be limited, focused, monopolized by a person, household, or group. This is important. My use of an item excludes your use. Autos, houses, food, electronics, air travel, concerts, massages, drugs, and so on.

Depletable means the benefit is consumed, or can be consumed, by the buyer, wearer, user, household, or individual.

Public goods are, to a greater or lesser extent, ***not*** excludable and ***not*** depletable. A good example is a road. A road is not depletable. No matter how many cars use a road today (and recognizing that there are limits to everything), cars will be using it tomorrow. A road is not excludable. Who will be able to collect a toll for every road? Who will be able to collect the cost of the service from the users if the road is plowed free of snow? Not being depletable means, in their own way, public goods are the goose that lays the golden egg. Once in place, or once delivered, a public good can produce benefits for years and years.

Not being exludable means the private market is unable to isolate the benefit sufficiently to be efficient in producing them. The private market requires payment in an amount approximating value. If that payment is too little, the market will produce too few. If that payment is too much, as when it is explicitly or implicitly subsidized, the market will produce too many. In a real sense, the market itself consists of nothing more or less than the moment of exchange, the moment of purchase and sale. Market participants may prepare years in advance, producing or earning the material of the exchange, but supply and demand and the market's price are determined at the point of this exchange.

The product of a public good, say national defense, is not excludable. If the nation, or my neighbor, is defended from attack, I am defended, even if I do not choose to pay for the service. The problem that quickly arises is known by the technical term the "free rider," and it is the reason the means of payment for public goods is universal and coercive — taxation. There ought to be no free riders on public goods. Since all benefit, the cost of the road, national defense and education ought to be shared by all.

To be clear, it is not because public goods are inferior in value, or somehow charity, that they are financed by taxation. Roads, police, education, public institutions are very good deals in cost-benefit terms and benefit those who are not direct users as well as those who are. This benefit is not retained in or somehow limited to the public sector.

MacDonald's founder Ray Kroc once asked his protégé, "*What business am I in?*" The unsurprising answer was, "*The restaurant business.*" Kroc corrected him, "*No. The real estate business.*" The value of Kroc's fast-food outlets depended on their location. The value of a location depends on access from streets and roads.

It is a surprise to nobody, perhaps, that a new highway or bridge may increase property values immensely. In some instances the road is tolled and part of the cost of its building is extracted from those who are direct users. But immense increases in property values may, and typically do, accrue to people who never use it. Decreased costs and expanded markets benefit a wide spectrum of economic actors and consumers, and these cannot be captured by a toll.

Does the same sort of benefit attend other public goods, say, education? Public education has an immense value, but that benefit is not monopolized by the individual. An education not expressed in family, community, or workplace is essentially valueless except as a source of amusement (or edification, to the more serious) for its owner. But when it is expressed in job earnings and spending, community and family, its benefits extend far beyond the individual — to the employer, the children, the neighbors and fellow citizens, and to the providers of goods and services. This benefit can be very great. The diffusion of beneficiaries is extended over the many years an education is used. A lifetime. It is easy to see that an education's value is not excludable, or in a sense, depletable. It is useful to consider education as one form of "social infrastructure."

Another form of social infrastructure is a stratum of public goods which does not cost as much as transportation infrastructure or national defense or public education, but which returns an enormous amount to the society. These are the political and legal organizing institutions. These institutions — legislatures, courts, the laws and adjudication of laws — provide an advantage to an economy proportionate to the degree of justice and fairness they provide. They provide common rules of the game which are indispensible. Nations with corrupted or non-functioning political and legal frameworks are often neo-feudal societies of oligarchs and strongmen. The relative cost of political and legal integrity is microscopic compared to its benefit.

These considerations indicate how government should organize its books. When looking at private sector balance sheets, economists have no difficulty seeing the two sides — assets and liabilities. If both sides are increased by the same amount, but the asset delivers a high rate of return, the balance sheet is stronger. Government balance sheets are the same. When the assets are public goods, which typically deliver high returns, the balance sheet can be stronger even when liabilities (debts) are larger. On the other hand, if borrowing by government is used simply to free up private spending, the balance sheet is weaker.

Taxation

Taxation is simply the means of purchasing or financing public goods, in the same way mortgages finance houses. Separating taxes from the public goods they purchase is an extremely effective political strategy to reduce government precisely because of the high returns to these goods. The strategy has become more and more successful since 1980. Taxes have become an evil in themselves, the fangs of a vampire government, money which disappears into a bloated bureaucracy, a theft of the necessary incentives to private activity. The goods themselves have become a given, or a reduction in them has been a sad but necessary act of prudent policy.

This may be a political win, but it is an economic failure. If it were true that taxes reduced well-being, then high tax countries or states would be the poorest, and those with the lowest taxes would be the richest. Somalia would be Sweden. The prosperity, stability and growth of the U.S. would have been greater in the era before 1940 and less afterward, because the rise of big government would have meant the end of prosperity. In fact, innovation and industrial development have flowered alongside the public sector. Automobiles needed interstate highways and a massive public road system. Aircraft, electronics and dozens of high tech advances needed the procurement and protection of the Defense Department. The Internet was not invented by far-seeing corporations moving into a promising new sphere, but by research under government auspices. Bio-tech companies now offer immense profitability as private operations, but are fundamentally spin-offs from research universities, both in personnel and projects. The contraction of support to public goods inevitably contracts an economy in the short run and true growth in the long run.

If you want a car with a smooth ride, you get a car loan for a BMW or Lexus. if you want a road with a smooth surface, you pay taxes. Nobody can buy a personal road with a credit card, any more than it would be appropriate for the government to purchase a BMW for an individual. A double-think has occurred. Taxes are evil and the services of government — one-third of all expenditures — are given. In fact, taxes are the mechanism of funding for public goods.

An ideal tax system would not distort economic incentives or market activity. Economists are nearly universal in wanting a low rate and a broad base for just this reason. They would like taxes to be a kind of overhead charge that affects every activity the same and so does not favor one enterprise over another. We are not going to go into detail in the present volume, but two important notes should be raised.

First, taxes can be used to correct for externalities. Costs that are not included in market prices because the seller does not bear responsibility for those costs can be replicated with a tax. Taxing cigarettes, gasoline, alcohol, and so on, can bring market prices in line with true product costs. This is not introducing a distortion, but correcting for one.

Second, the tax system in the United States bears little resemblance to this low rate, broad base ideal, nor is it particularly progressive, as many have argued. The federal personal income tax is complicated, rife with loopholes, exclusions and preferences, and treats people in fundamentally the same circumstances differently. Economists would say it lacks both horizontal and vertical equity. The payroll tax, the largest in terms of revenue generation, is patently regressive. Earnings subject to the tax are capped (at $110,000 in 2012), meaning the effective rate is lower as income rises. Many kinds of income are excluded entirely from the payroll tax, e.g., capital gains, interest income and rents. The corporate income tax generates barely ten percent of total federal revenues, when in the 1950s it produced about fifty percent. It is more of a book of subsidies than a means of efficiently generating revenue.[1]

---

[1] State and local taxes are primarily personal income (derived from federal tax returns), property, and sales or excise taxes. These fund a great portion of the direct services received by the public, from schools to police and fire protection, to roads and libraries.

Natural Monopolies

Related to, but not identical with, public goods are *natural monopolies*. These are spheres of the economy which are made less efficient by competition — sewer, water, power, landline telephone, garbage collection, services which require cable or piping, health care, and many forms of social insurance, including retirement and disability insurance, even rail transportation. The connection is often close between natural monopolies and public goods.

But the main reason it is useful and common for the public sector to be intimately involved in managing natural monopolies is that they escape the discipline of a competitive market. The efficiency is to scale, and sooner or later they will come to be run by a single entity and will be able to exploit the monopoly's pricing power. Profits will be extracted that are not available to market-based sectors, and so will not be set at efficient or reasonable levels.

In some cases, government or quasi-government agencies provide these services directly. In others, private providers are closely regulated. Utility rates typically adhere to strict regulatory guidelines. Cable companies get close local government scrutiny. Electricity comes in by either public or private lines, but is organized by the public sector. Water, garbage, and so on, are not advertised on television. These industries are potentially massively profitable to a private corporation. But profits and efficiency are not sacrificed when the industry is managed by the public. Instead they are spread, as reduced prices or broader delivery areas mean lower costs to private actors, and profits accrue to them, just as with public goods.

It is no accident that the privatization we saw in our chapter on Globalization with Joseph Stiglitz is popular with the corporate oligarchy and natural monopolies. It is also no accident that privatization is adopted more readily in less developed locales and under the IMF mandates than in states and nations with robust political institutions.

The capture of the regulators is often the path to private control in the more advanced states. When railroads, insurance companies, banks, electricity providers, media conglomerates and the rest can convince their regulators that higher prices or concessionary terms are necessary for optimal efficiency, they have control of demand. The convincing is much easier when the regulators are appointed from the ranks of the regulated by political representatives that are beholden to the regulated. This "captured regulator" is a signal aspect of James K. Galbraith's Predator State.

When, on the other hand, natural monopolies operate for the benefit of the society as a whole, costs are reduced for private actors, but service can also be managed for long-term goals. Electricity generated by coal or natural gas, for example, is often more cheap or profitable only because the costs of global warming are not included in the price. We look at this in the next chapter. Or railroads which target long-haul or bulk transport because that is where the profits are can be encouraged or required to provide short-haul and passenger transport, which are more efficient uses of infrastructure.

Monopolies are often thought of as a failure of the market that ought to be corrected, but natural monopolies are not a failure, just a fact of economic life. It is no more reasonable to encourage competition in this area than it is to encourage competition in road construction.

The Commons

The "Tragedy of the Commons" threatens to become the tragedy of the human race. The archetype for this metaphor was the Commons of 17th Century Scotland, where pasture outside the boundaries of private property was available for all to graze their cattle. This valuable resource dissolved by over-use. Without a hand to control it, and without incentive to restrict use at the individual level, the Commons became overgrazed and barren. The resource was depleted even as the cattle became gaunt and useless.

The solution to the problem was the triumph of private property. When the Commons was enclosed and put under control of the local lord, who then had the incentive to manage it responsibly, both cattle and pasture improved and prospered. Unfortunately, many of the farmer-users of the Commons did not share in the prosperity, and were forced into tenancy or into the squalid cities of the Industrial Revolution.

Economics as theory has yet to bridge the gap to the real world in terms of the global natural Commons. It is stuck in the virtue of private property. Global warming and climate change proceed apace. The incentive to manage responsibly the common resources of air, water, soil and natural systems remains locked outside the perquisites of private control. The Commons of the planet are exploited, polluted, denuded and exhausted in the name of economic efficiency, when it is not efficiency, but unfettered access that is creating profits.

The modern Commons resist enclosure, and attempts to manage them for the common good and long-term efficiency is confounded by the power of the entrenched interests. The regulator, the fence, is not established. The economic momentum, in fact, is in the opposite direction and means resources and systems will deteriorate and ultimately fail.

Here we see a dynamic reminiscent of public goods, the "free rider." The one who can evade control will prosper, at least in the short term. The responsible will be exploited by the irresponsible unless all are brought under a single framework. Control, restriction, lease of the opportunity to use the Commons are possible, because they are essential to planetary survival. The private interests of the current users and the disparate interests of the national governments need to be offset by a new regime at least at the level of property rights.

Public goods, natural monopolies, and the Commons bring economics back into the real world from its illusions of market efficiency. Market efficiency is patently nonexistent in these areas. But the transition from current economic theory to a more complete view which includes these realities is frustrated not only by the self-interest of oil companies, but by the fog of distorted measurement and the innate blindness of the Market. We will take these up in the next chapter. First we turn to another concept — the multiplier.

Multiplier

In studying demand, John Maynard Keynes adopted the "multiplier" being developed by R.F. Kahn. This is the factor by which an initial direct demand stimulus can be multiplied to gauge ultimate total demand. The following is necessarily theoretical and may be complicated for the average reader, but the multiplier is very poorly understood and poorly used in modern economics. By understanding it, the reader will be able to judge likely impacts of various policy choices.

The principle Kahn explored is straightforward. An investment or government expenditure creates a series of echoes, as the same money is spent over and over by subsequent participants. Income is spent and becomes income to another. The workers and contractors who produce one good consume others. That income is used by the producers of those in the same way. Nobody carries his paycheck away and hides it from the world. Instead it is used to buy food and shelter and clothing, as well as to pay taxes to buy schools and national defense and other public goods.

Thus the same dollar is spent several times. The sequence stops only when one or another actor saves instead of spends. So any particular amount of government spending or private investment that is new to the economy will create multiples of that amount in economic activity. The multiplier is the number of times that dollar of income is spent.[2]

---

[2] There are many multipliers the reader may encounter, most of which are not this Keynesian investment multiplier. One of them is the money multiplier, which is the expression of the fallacy of exogenous money we explored with Minsky. That is, the idea that so-called "base money" created by the central bank is passively multiplied by the

If all actors had the same propensity to save, the multiplier would be the reciprocal of the savings rate. So if, say, each actor saved 5 percent of her income, the multiplier should be 20. There is a problem. The observed multiplier is closer to 2 than 20. That is, when economists mine data in the real world, they do not find large multipliers. This empirical evidence has been used by some to indicate the multiplier does not exist, rather than that it is much lower than would be expected from the superficial math. Since Algebra would have to be refuted, we look for another explanation.

One favorite explanation from the orthodoxy is that there is no new spending possible, particularly from government. The reasoning runs that if government spends, then it must borrow from the private sector the amount that is spent. Thus the effect is perfectly offset between one person's spending and another's not spending. That is, the money used to spend on, say, a government contract, must have come from money available to other activities. This "crowding out" theory did not withstand the experience of the Great Financial Crisis.

Another argument in this line is that if government cuts taxes to stimulate private demand, individuals will realize that they will be on the hook for tax rises in the futures and will save just that amount. This "Ricardian equivalence" theory was a favorite of the Rational Expectations school. It has been contradicted by evidence that people do not save against future tax increases, and by the obvious limitation that individuals have life spans which limit their liability for taxes, so that the "rational" will not save.

More to the point, as we have seen, borrowing in the private sector is not dependent on savers, but on the willingness of bankers. This is particularly true of borrowing that is done to finance entrepreneurial development. (Kahn's notion was originally called the "investment multiplier.") The same independence from savers exists for government. More and more of the federal debt is owned by the Fed, and in theory, the government could simply credit accounts without borrowing.[3]

---

banking system. We saw that money is, in fact, produced in the process of lending, not prior to lending, and later base money is ratified by the central bank. Another form of multiplier is the input-output (I/O) multiplier, an elaborate matrix of connections between supply-side sectors. The I/O multiplier attempts to translate an investment by means of its effects on other sectors. For example, if a new factory is built to manufacture wood products, it will increase activity in lumber, transportation, retail, distribution, machine tools, etc., in some proportion that is derived by empirical study. That proportion is assumed to remain stable. Unfortunately the process is always in flux by technology or geography, and the results are often far different than the estimates, a phenomenon which always seems to take government officials who rely on the predictions by surprise.

[3] Modern Monetary Theory espouses just such a tack, creating spending without increasing the debt load, and dealing with inflation when it appears by tax policy. The

Turning to more legitimate explanations for differences between a high theoretical and a low empirical multiplier:

First, not all actors have the same propensity to save. The lower the income, in fact, the lower the propensity to save. The top one percent of income earners save 25 percent of their incomes. The bottom — at least until recently — save a negative amount. The dampening effect on the multiplier when 20 percent of income goes to the top one percent is obvious.

Second, for debt payments, the money has already been spent. Debt payments are like savings in that they kill the echo of the multiplier. Consumer credit, household mortgages, student loans, are increases to demand when they are taken out, but decreases to demand when they are paid back. It explains why the change in credit is so effective in stimulating demand, and why there is a hangover from debt binges that is more serious than many account for.

Third, a recipient of the income may choose to spend it on products from outside the economy, imports, in which case the trailing echoes may belong to another society. In situations where trade is balanced, of course, there would be a commensurate demand returning to the first economy. Where trade is not balanced — that is, where demand for foreign goods is not balanced by demand for domestic goods — the exercise simply increases debt and depresses the multiplier.

Fourth, some products that are not in themselves imported are so capital- or resource-intensive — and thus the proportion of labor income in them is so much smaller than others — that they are a serious drag on the multiplier. This is particularly true of energy (oil) throughout its supply chain, from extraction through distribution and retail.

On the other hand, Demand Side does not deduct taxes from the multiplier. It is the Demand Side view that taxes typically go either to direct transfers to others — as in the case of payroll taxes in the U.S. — or to workers with fairly low propensities to save.

If we trace the typical patterns of spending and the factors that reduce the multiplier, we see that the main weighting is added in the first and second steps, or echoes. A sequence of spending might run as follows: Investment to Contractor (minus profit and fixed costs) to Worker (minus savings, house payment, net consumer debt) to Consumer Goods Producers (minus profit, fixed costs, imports, oil) to Consumer Goods Workers (minus savings, house payments, net consumer debt) ... and so on.

---

theory survives logical and theoretical scrutiny, but the practice may be prohibited by the politics and the citizen's intuitive conservative bias.

Figure 13-1

Fiscal Stimulus Bang for the Buck

Tax Cuts	Bang for the Buck
Non-refundable Lump-Sum Tax Rebate	1.01
Refundable Lump-Sum Tax Rebate	1.22
Temporary Tax Cuts	
Payroll Tax Holiday	1.24
Job Tax Credit	1.30
Across the Board Tax Cut	1.02
Accelerated Depreciation	0.25
Loss Carryback	0.22
Housing Tax Credit	0.90
Permanent Tax Cuts	
Extend Alternative Minimum Tax Patch	0.51
Make Bush Income Tax Cuts Permanent	0.32
Make Dividend and Capital Gains Tax Cuts Permanent	0.37
Cut in Corporate Tax Rate	0.32

Spending Increases	Bang for the Buck
Extending Unemployment Insurance Benefits	1.61
Temporary Federal Financing of Work-Share Programs	1.69
Temporary Increase in Food Stamps	1.74
General Aid to State Governments	1.41
Increased Infrastructure Spending	1.57
Low Income Home Energy Assistance Program (LIHEAP)	1.13

Note: The bang for the buck is estimated by the one year $ change in GDP for a given $ reduction in federal tax revenue or increase in spending.

Source: Moody's Analytics (Blinder & Zandi, 2010)

Estimates of the effective multiplier can be obtained either from the theoretical side, as we have done, or from the empirical side. One such empirically derived table was developed by Mark Zandi, and we reproduce it in Figure 13-1. This "Bang for the Buck" table was produced for an analysis of the **American Recovery and Reinvestment Act** (the so-called "Obama Stimulus") and associated activities. This is a very conservative set of multipliers.[4]

The smaller weighting for tax cuts, as opposed to infrastructure or aid to

---

[4] One must note the vigorous condemnation even these very conservative numbers drew from the anti-tax market fundamentalists. Although Zandi was noted for his advisory role to Republican presidential candidates, the observation that tax cuts were significantly less useful to economic stimulus than spending increases was not consistent with the conservative beliefs of that party.

states, reflects another wrinkle in the multiplier. While a $100,000 spending increase may be the same in terms of government borrowing, it will have a different effect depending on the uses of the primary recipient. Tax cuts for many types of investment will not translate into new spending unless the profit potential is there — which means the demand for the investment is there — although it may bring forward in time the new investment. Tax cuts to individuals may well produce an increase in consumer demand, but that increase will be concentrated in a narrow segment of consumption, primarily consumer discretionaries.

This is what was in evidence, though not observed by many, with the tax provisions of the Bush 2008 stimulus program and the subsequent 2009 tax provisions. That is, for example, a 2 percent payroll tax reduction was expressed in the economy primarily as spending on consumer discretionaries, including energy, and on paying down debt. Were the same number of dollars used to directly hire people, as in the case of public works, it would affect fewer initial recipients, but result in a much broader spectrum of spending. A job produces demand for housing, consumer durables, child care, etc., that a small addition to many paychecks cannot replicate. (Direct job creation also means new job-holders pay taxes, and so the net cost of the program is lower.)

This is a good example. Approximately $480 billion was needed to fund the payroll tax holiday in 2012. If this were instead dedicated to direct job creation, it could fund ten million jobs at $48,000 per year. This would obviously eliminate the unemployment problem, and the $80 billion or more in new federal tax receipts would partially offset the cost. (Also offsetting the cost would be the reduction in spending on unemployment benefits and the need for other social safety net programs.) But the multiplier effect would likely be nearly as large as the initial, direct effect, as new demand for goods and services across the economy generated jobs elsewhere.

The high multiplier numbers in Zandi's table for state and local government services reflect the large number of jobs per dollar of spending in these services. This multiplier is already near 1.0 before the first echo of spending. The smaller results for tax cuts reflects the considerations above. The differences can be massive. Support for states and localities has a multiplier almost five times that of cuts in corporate tax rates.

All of this is theoretical foundation for what we should expect from the multiplier. There are other applications that should not be missed.

The multiplier will change depending on the economic context. When the debt load of households is high or economic prospects for households are uncertain, their propensity to spend will be lower, and their choices of what goods to buy will be different. If income disparities grow, and more income is concentrated among the wealthy, who have a lower propensity to spend out of income, the multiplier will be depressed. The spending of the wealthy, in fact, may not be affected at all by changes in income, because their spending comes out of accumulated wealth, not incremental income. Changes in income may be used simply to bid up asset prices.

The disparity between effective multipliers for different groups means, however, that it is not necessary for the spending increase to come from entirely outside the system — to be truly exogenous — to have a positive effect. If one group has a higher effective multiplier, simply transferring income to them from a group with a lower multiplier will stimulate the economy with no other change or net cost. In our example, if money were moved from corporate taxes into state and local government spending, we should expect at least a four-fold increase in economic activity. This is known as the "balanced budget multiplier," taxing the rich to support investment. Stiglitz estimates the number at 2.0-3.0. (Stiglitz J. , 2011) That is, *since the multiplier changes in relation to the distribution of income, policies which favor more equal distribution will tend to be more economically efficient.*

Other policy implications we can distill from this discussion:

The multiplier ratifies stimulus in the form of public works projects, as Keynes originally proposed. When government services produce five times the bang for the buck that can be found from some tax cuts, the economic argument is closed, however much the political argument may be enlivened.

Energy conservation and retrofitting, if they are replacements for purchases from resourced-based capital-intensive industries like oil will have a stimulative effect. This is contrary, of course, to the notion that "We cannot afford to fix the energy problem." Projects which substitute energy efficiency for energy consumption will increase the multiplier, not just save the future. This is a permanently higher multiplier, not just on the front end with the labor involved in installation of solar panels or insulation, but in the long term as well, as spending is freed to more labor-intensive products.

Reducing debt loads will increase the multiplier. Programs that, for example, facilitate principle reduction in home mortgages — regardless of their impact on lenders — will increase spending in the aggregate unless they discourage net lending in the future.

Before we leave the multiplier, it is important to be clear that the economic vitality captured by this concept is not the same as the boom and bust related to bubbles and debt expansion. Quite the reverse. Ponzi asset price bubbles may induce investment and create self-reinforcing booms for a time, but this comes from debt-driven demand. Eventually the debt must be repaid, which reduces the multiplier and the vitality of the economy, particularly when such investment does not create value commensurate with the debt.. Public works or private investment projects which are not Ponzi in nature, on the other hand, may increase the multiplier by freeing spending power. That is, investment may produce value in terms of efficiencies. As costs for, say, transportation come down, more may be spent on food or day care. This is separate and distinct from whatever demand stimulus may derive from the initial investments.

With these concepts in mind, we turn to the problem and opportunity of the Market.

Chapter 14:

Making Markets Work

> *Faced with the choice between changing one's mind*
> *and proving that there is no need to do so, almost everyone*
> *gets busy on the proof.*
>
> John Kenneth Galbraith

Private competitive markets are dynamic, efficient mechanisms for creating and distributing goods and services to meet effective demand. Capitalist economies with functioning markets can produce the most at the least cost and distribute that product precisely where it is demanded, given certain assumptions.

This statement is one with which most economists would agree. But does such a competitive market exist today? ***Can*** markets work as advertised? It has been a purpose of this book to define the actual economy as a corporate oligarchy which operates under the mantle of market fundamentalism. This regime seeks to control markets, regulation, policy and politics even as it espouses a religion of freedom and non-interference. In this chapter we look at how markets operate in theory and how they might be structured to work in practice.

Promote and Maintain Adequate Demand, Incomes and Investment

Markets must have adequate effective demand as a base. First and last, public policy should promote full employment. As the preceding chapter demonstrated, it is possible to have a fully employed economy producing value if we are willing to organize and plan. Leaving to the private sector the provision of demand, the levels of incomes and the choices of investment is leaving our economy to the manipulation of entrenched interests.

We have shown there are no theoretical constraints to achieving this first principle. Rather, the constraints are political, academic and financial — the "institutional" constraints of the Galbraiths, elder and younger. A Demand Side economic policy will remain theoretical, an intellectual window on the possible, so long as it cannot be instituted on the ground. And it is an open issue how soon that day will arrive. But economics needs not only theory, but political position from which to operate, and pragmatic results to reinforce public support. That position is not now in prospect. Control of policy levers by entrenched interests — academic, political and financial — is firm. The current public support of demand and investment is ad hoc: (1) high government deficits to finance tax cuts to promote consumer and business spending, and (2) ever lower interest rates combined with extraordinary tax concessions to support investment. The program is a manifest failure. Higher debt, lower incomes, distorted financial markets and constricted channels for recovery — all of these stem from the solutions of the orthodoxy, not from the original problems.

I am sometimes asked, "Can't we just cut back?" Well, we can cut back, each of us individually. This is no doubt the rational thing to do when faced with declining earnings, heavier debt loads and questions about the future. But cutting back will not help the economy. We are faced with inadequate effective demand, and this is not cured by reducing demand further. This is the **paradox of thrift**. Prudent and frugal and sustainable behavior by the individual adds up to less produce and economic activity for the whole, and inevitably filters back down to spur another round of cutting back. But it is not the role of the individual to take it upon herself to spend, spend, spend for the good of society. It is certainly not the call of self-interest in the face of questions about the future. This is the role of public policy — to fill the demand gap with productive, targeted investment and employment programs. Putting a floor under incomes, promoting financial security among its citizens, and offering a clear direction for development. This is the regimen that will lead naturally to sturdy consumer demand and productive business opportunities.

So now having gotten to step one, adequate effective demand, let us look again at our paragraph:

Private competitive markets are dynamic, efficient mechanisms for creating and distributing goods and services to meet effective demand. Capitalist economies with functioning markets can produce the most at the least cost and distribute that product precisely where it is demanded, given certain assumptions.

We begin with the definitions and assumptions needed to make this statement true and useful. We find the assumptions more heroic than reasonable. We then look at the problems of measurement; GDP growth is a very poor estimation of an economy's health or a society's well-being, yet it is the primary metric for most economists. Finally, we examine the limitations of markets in terms of efficiency, foresight and adequacy, and look at which market structures do actually work.

Competitive Markets.

An accepted definition of competitive markets would begin: a market of *many producers*, none of whom can influence the price (these are "*price takers*"), all of whom produce a *product that is comparable* to the others, where there is little difficulty for new producers to enter the market (low "*barriers to entry*"), and one in which buyers and sellers have comparable knowledge of the product ("*symmetric information*"). If such a market existed, it would no doubt generate optimal outcomes for consumers. But it does not exist, except on the smallest scale. The reason is that such markets are competed away. In every instance, profit disappears when markets are competitive. A good example of this is Agriculture. American farmers are the most efficient in the world in terms of producing agricultural commodities, but the early historical experience of standard product, low barriers to entry, population of price takers, and symmetric information was to create a market that drove farmers into bankruptcy. Only when cooperatives, government subsidies and artificial crop restrictions were added was the damage of a competitive market mitigated. This experience is sometimes excused, sometimes ignored by market fundamentalists.

Every single tenet of competitive market theory is violated in practice. Corporations seek "pricing power," either in the form of control of demand or restriction of supply. Successful companies are not price takers; they seek to differentiate their product from others, to avoid direct competition. This is true down to the smallest retail level, where identical convenience stores will not exist on the same street, but will differentiate by location. (It is true that malls will congregate big box retailers or one area will house a number of restaurants, but this might be seen as a form of cooperation to attract shoppers, not competition in our strict definition.)

Low barriers to entry do exist in some business sectors, where know-how, energy and vision may give opportunity to the small-scale capitalist. But expansion becomes a matter of credit. An entrepreneur is first a person who can borrow. Many industries — including most of the largest — are completely controlled by a few dominant corporations. The path to success for a newcomer in such industries is to create a niche in the market and hope to be bought out.

As to perfect information, Joseph Stiglitz received a Nobel Prize for his work in demonstrating that asymmetrical information is the norm, not the exception. By this measure alone, competitive markets do not exist.[1]

This is not to say that competition does not exist. Many large markets see fierce competition between large corporations. Leaving aside the obviously huge barriers to entry, these markets may appear at first to be competitive by the classical definition. Ford does indeed compete with General Motors and Nissan and Honda. The companies compete for customers, but they act together to expand and protect the automobile industry as a whole, and they act in concert with oil companies and satellite industries to protect and promote auto-based transportation. Historically, they promoted and defended the public goods needed for highways to replace railways. Fundamental to the growth of the industry was the federal Interstate Highway System produced under the premise of national defense in the **National Interstate and Defense Highways Act of 1956**. Charles E. Wilson, formerly CEO of General Motors, was the Secretary of Defense at the time.[2] (Equally instructive was the secret purchase of streetcar companies across the nation by GM in the period from 1936 to 1950. After the companies were bought out, the tracks were torn up and the provision of service was either abandoned or turned to rubber-tired buses. (Competition was better in theory than practice.)

It has been a theme of this book that large corporations control demand, capture government and arrange their markets to produce what they want to produce. Indeed, considering the huge investments they must make in plant, equipment, and human resources, it would be irrational to do otherwise. But it is not reasonable to call the resulting system a competitive or free market. Such arrangements lead to overproduction and overconsumption of everything from automobiles to debt, and cannot be sustained or stable.

---

[1] Buyers — the demand side — cannot assess the value or nature of the product or service as well as the sellers — the suppliers. The implications range beyond the occasional product liability suit or unhappy customer. A relevant cause — indeed, a root cause — of the housing bubble and subsequent bust of the early 2000s was the practice by mortgage originators to systematically hide or disguise terms of loans that later exploded in the faces of borrowers in the form of rate resets or balloon payments. The market is not efficient if the buyer and seller are not negotiating a price for the same thing.

[2] Wilson is famous, or infamous, for his reported observation to a Congressional committee: "What is good for GM is good for the United States, and *vice versa.*

Measurement

A healthy economy has come to mean one with an expanding GDP — gross domestic product is growing. *Change* in GDP determines recession or recovery in the minds of economists. This leads to some confusion in translation to the public, which is more interested in the *level* of GDP. An economy can deteriorate in terms of product from a very high level, and the public will think things are still okay, but the economist will see recession. An economy can improve very slightly from a deep trough — again in terms of product — with its public sector borrowing huge sums, its unemployment rate in at epidemic levels and its household incomes stagnant. The public will be alarmed, but the economist will see recovery. The difference is the difference between level and change.

Beyond this, however, the metric of GDP itself is deeply flawed, and it does not represent the health or sustainability of the economy very well. As developed by Simon Kuznets in the 1930s, the **National Income and Product Accounts** were enabled by the conceptual advances of John Maynard Keynes and the Demand Siders. These measurements have not been altered in any fundamental form in more than half a century. In these NIPA accounts, GDP equals GDI, Gross Domestic Product equals Gross Domestic Income, and the accounting philosophy is slanted to a pre-war manufacturing model.

The first problem is that GDP measures only monetized activity. Restaurant meals are in, meals at home are not. The reduction of reserves of oil and gas by their sale is in; depletion of air, soil and water is out. The product of factories and farms is in. The product of roads and schools is out. An accurate measurement of economic vitality would account for the depletion of the Commons and the exhaustion of natural systems and resources. Depletion and depreciation are established in current macroeconomic accounts only for private economic actors. Likewise, public goods and public investment are mentioned in GDP only in terms of spending, not product or service. Roads, education, the skills of a labor market, public goods of all kinds, the Commons — all are excluded.

The second problem is that GDP measures activity, not outcomes or products. A home is the equivalent of jail, nutrition the equivalent of alcoholism, education the equivalent of pornography. "Goods" are the equivalent of "bads." GDP measures the buzzing around the hive rather than the honey inside, or the strength of the structure of the hive, or even the health of the queen. A heart rate or blood pressure reading is not necessarily related to good health. Neither is GDP. The very acts that destroy the future — wars, pollution, crime, financial bubbles — are additions to GDP. An inefficient economic activity, such as the U.S. health care system, is twice as valuable in terms of GDP as the systems of other nations which produce better outcomes at lower costs. If outcomes of health care were the measure of product, by this means alone, GDP in the U.S. would be between roughly 5 and 7 percent below its published level. If an accounting for goods vs. bads were done, it is likely that simply by deducting for things such as high levels of incarceration, social and public health dysfunction and military spending, the GDP measure would be at least another 5 percent below its official rendering. (This perhaps comes as no surprise to travelers to Europe or Japan who see conditions and standards of living that seem to be superior in nations with lower GDP.)

A third problem is that investment in public goods is treated differently than investment in private goods. Most often it is ignored. Public investment is treated in GDP accounting, as in political discourse, predominantly as spending. Investment in private goods is valued at a high level, promoted by tax rules and often carried on accounts at inflated values.

These measurement problems do not lie in the difficulties of assessing true well-being of citizens or the monetary value of public goods or the Commons. An excellent beginning to revised national accounting was produced in a report under the leadership of Nobel laureates Joseph Stiglitz and Amartya Sen in 2009. (Sarkozy Commission, 2009) The Sarkozy Commission identified the issues and highlighted the best thinking on them. Measurements as currently contrived promote consumption and private goods and discount social and environmental costs. Accurate metrics are not so much opposed by entrenched interests, including orthodox economics, as they are ignored.

Income Equality.

In the conventional consideration of output, goods and bads are treated equally. This means output does not reflect well-being or value. More equal societies create more goods than bads, and we should then rate them higher than those which are unequal. This is over and above and separate from any value judgment as to justice or fairness. That is, we are talking about economic efficiency, not redistributive justice. The point is well drawn by Richard Wilkinson and Kate Pickett in their research and book *The Spirit Level*. (Wilkinson & Pickett, 2009) Societies with more equal distribution of incomes experience significantly better outcomes in an extraordinary range of socioeconomic measures. Trust, teenage pregnancy rates, social mobility, anxiety, obesity, health outcomes, incarceration, crime, and dozens of other conditions are more favorable in societies with more equal incomes. This is true whether that equality has been achieved by redistribution through the tax system, as in Sweden, or whether the pre-tax distribution is more equal, as in Japan.

Because of the statistically demonstrable benefits to income equality — a greater percentage of GDP composed of goods and less in bads — more equal societies ought to be recognized as more efficient. GDP is an advantage in being an aggregate measure, but aggregation does not require obtuseness. It is a simple matter to factor for income equality.[3]

This is a rather superficial treatment of the problem of measurement, but it demonstrates at a minimum that GDP alone is a poor gauge of economic outcomes or efficiency. Now let us return, however briefly and inadequately, to the question of market efficiency on more theoretical grounds.

Investment

Beyond the need for specific products is the need for investment in industry and infrastructure that is compatible with social and environmental stability. The current industrial base and technology is weighted heavily to fossil fuels and intensive use of energy. Building new systems will require creative destruction on a grand scale, not the petty private market creative destruction of Schumpeter.[4] It is the remaking of transportation and housing infrastructure, reconstruction of energy production and distribution systems, and a reorganization of Agriculture around the world. Not a small undertaking and well beyond the scope of this volume. We isolate here "investment" as a market in need of structure. As we saw from Minsky, stable investment can be found only in hedge financing — financing based on a stream of value created from that investment.

---

[3] Wilkinson and Pickett replicated their analysis with U.S. states, and again found the pattern. More equal incomes produced better outcomes across the board.

[4] "Creative destruction" is a term well loved by market fundamentalists as a virtue of innovation and the inherent devaluing of previous technologies (or even downsizing companies). It is now primarily associated with Joseph Schumpeter and the Austrian School. Originally used and developed by Karl Marx, creative destruction was a concept to describe the innate inability of capitalism to control or mitigate the destruction and devaluation of productive forces by way of economic crises, neglect, war, or another mechanism. Even Schumpeter's view was hardly benign: "That process, impressive in its relentless necessity, was not merely a matter of removing institutional deadwood, but of removing partners of the capitalist stratum, symbiosis with whom was an essential element of the capitalist schema." (Schumpeter J., 1942, p. 142) In our use here, we refer to the essential replacement of a carbon-intensive society by an environmentally sustainable one, in terms of infrastructure, energy use, urban design, and so on. Whether the massive destruction of productive capital and labor is essential to capitalism in theory or not, it is evident in practice. No more so than in the current time, when, however, resistance by those displaced is extremely strong.

Financing for consumption or for Ponzi speculation obviously does not create the stream of value out of which debt can be serviced, and so is unstable. Investment in facilities and infrastructure which prolong the habitable life of the planet or improve social security and welfare do increase real value, in a way easily understood by the lay person. It is the task of economics to create structures that monetize that value and make it accessible to investors.

For example, a next-generation direct current electrical grid (as advocated by NASA's James Hansen) could link renewable energy sources around the continent to energy consumers without transmission losses. This would reduce delivery prices of alternatives and make investments in renewables attractive to private developers. The grid itself is a public good, a natural monopoly, of such a size and with such diverse beneficiaries that only the public sector will undertake its construction. The value of this good, however, and its financing can be made available to private investors. An infrastructure bond, yielding a good rate, is simple to construct and guarantee. Investors buy municipal bonds on a greater scale which have less apparent values. The value is obvious and only needs to be monetized.

Structuring the Market

In most treatments of markets and capitalism, there is a section entitled "Market Failures," which covers things like monopolies, externalities, or remedies in the case of any violation of the assumptions we explored at the beginning of this chapter. The premise is that markets tend toward the most efficient outcome, led by the invisible hand of self-interest. Demand Side takes an alternative view. Markets are inherently unstable and prone to excess. In order to reap the benefits from their power and efficiency, markets must be **structured** so they bring their theoretical advantages into practice. Market discipline can be counted on only in more or less competitive markets. Some spheres of activity that cannot be structured into markets must be controlled by the public sector or use auction markets. Control cannot be abdicated to the private sector. The inherent blindness of markets to the future and their inability to provide the aggregate demand upon which they depend must be remedied by public investment and management.

We will cover this enormous range of inquiry in a short section of one chapter. These are ways to make markets work.

Incorporate costs into prices.

Unless the costs of externalities can be incorporated into the market price of goods, the price will not be efficient, so the market will not be efficient. The term "externality" applies to costs of a good or service not borne by the market's buyers or sellers, but instead absorbed by the public sector or the Commons. The use of oil and gasoline, for example, creates enormous environmental damage and future liabilities, but as soon as the price is paid at the pump, the market is done with its accounting for the costs. As we suggested in the last chapter, the costs shift to the public sector and future generations. A tax could be a surrogate for some of this cost. This is the practice in Europe today. But in the U.S. the gasoline tax is dedicated completely to the construction of roads, which are economically simply the means for maximum consumption of the gasoline. (Some states apply additional sales tax, but even these revenues likely do not cover policing, traffic management and emergency services, also internal to the use of the gasoline.) It is entirely appropriate to levy taxes as proxies for costs.[5] To close the loop, net revenues from additional externality taxes would be allocated to environmental remedies, but market efficiency demands only that the taxes approximate those costs and bring the pricing into line with those costs.

Similarly, the cost of the casino in financial markets is enormous, yet there is no accounting for this in the price of transactions. A tiny transactions tax (sometimes called the "Tobin Tax" after James Tobin who first proposed it) would be invisible to real economic activity. It could be levied at one dollar for every two thousand dollars (.05 percent). But because speculation and purely financial games involve the movement of such massive amounts of money repeatedly, and the tax would be levied at each transaction, it would fall much heavier on the activity not integral to the real economy. The revenue could be enormous, but perhaps more beneficial would be the reduction in profit from what is essentially nonproductive and destabilizing speculation.

Standardize products and services.

A competitive market needs to have multiple producers of a single product in order for competition to create the highest welfare at the lowest price. It is the ambition of each firm on the supply side to differentiate its product from the field or to monopolize its market to achieve pricing power and thus maximum profit. Monopoly power is widely recognized and regulated, though often not effectively. Differentiation is another matter. Making one's product different can, on one hand, benefit consumers in terms of choice. On the other hand, and with

---

[5] An intriguing method to bring the cost into the price was proposed in 2010 in the U.S. Senate. The Cantwell-Collins bill would have restricted the sale of oil more and more each year, and required the sellers to bid for authority to sell. The revenue from this auction would have been returned to the population on a per capita basis. Thus the consuming public would have been made financially whole, and in most cases more than whole, but the market would have altered the price in line with the cost.

the example of the financial sector in mind, differentiation can be a means to obscuration and frustration of symmetrical information. Standardizing mortgages, credit cards and other financial products can allow true competition. To the extent that products are differentiated simply in order to destroy comparison and hence competition, the market is not efficient.

Segregate natural monopolies.

The price charged for the output of natural monopolies must be strictly controlled, because these monopolies have no competitive restraints. One dominant provider will always rise, and absent artificial restrictions, will extract wealth from the economy in proportion to its position, not to the value of its product. Thus natural monopolies are often closely regulated. Publicly owned utilities price at the cost of production. Privately owned utilities are strictly monitored by rate-setting commissions or processes. Some natural monopolies do exist outside direct government control. Rail transportation in the U.S. is one example. Since the services of these natural monopolies are essential for all, it is essential also to make sure they are available for all.

Eliminate tax preferences for demand manipulation.

Lobbying, advertising beyond basic information, capture of regulators, skyboxes at football games, and on and on into a host of sales and marketing endeavors, are not costs of production and distribution, but of manipulating demand. It is understandable that corporations which have invested large sums want to assure a steady stream of demand. They want to assure the stream of returns to pay off sometimes very large commitments. But insofar as the market is controlled by anything other than supply and demand, the market is not efficient. A market controlled by lobbying or advertising or bribery is a market of information or persuasion, not a market of goods and services. Subsidizing these efforts through the tax code is unnecessary.

Restrict the size of market participants.

Avoiding "too big to fail" and closely monitoring monopolies and oligopolies is a practice that arose in response to the Robber Barons of the 19th Century. But in the aftermath of the Great Financial Crisis, the lesson was lost. The size of banking institutions became a rationale for public underwriting, not a distortion to be remedied. Too big to fail banks have grown ever larger in size since the Great Financial Crisis and continue to receive preference from the central bank and government. There is no natural monopoly in banking. That is, there is no efficiency of scale. Banking is a one-on-one business. It operates best with close relationships. When the banking industry became dominated by a few megabanks, it was not from efficiency of lending, but from mismanagement of risk and a move into non-bank activities like trading and derivatives. Unfortunately, the core credit creation function and the payment system are largely under control of these banks. A breakdown in these vital functions was feared by regulators, so the banks were absolved of market discipline when they failed. Too big to fail is too big to exist in a private market.

Align management incentives with company interests.

Corporations are often dominated by management teams that have very short-term orientations. The profit motive is a powerful motive. Unfortunately, to the market fundamentalist, it is the primary virtue. Greed is literally good. The promise of riches brings out the best in people, it is argued, and produces the best outcomes for the society. This dynamic is essential for the invisible hand to work. We have shown that if the invisible hand exists, it is blind with regard to the the larger interests of society. But even the well-being of shareholder-owners can be served only if the financial interests of the company and those of its management are aligned. A Coca-Cola or GE may be perceived to be a long-term, forward-looking organization, but because remuneration is often based on the current price of the stock, the time horizon is much shorter for its managers — the next quarter, the next earning statement.[6] So decisions are made, as John Kenneth Galbraith noted decades ago, recognizing *"... the stockholder ... is a passive and functionless figure."* The process has only deteriorated since then.

Eliminate subsidies and tax preferences.

"Industrial policy" is an economic code term often used disparagingly for picking winners and losers, or selecting target industries and sectors to promote at the expense of others. We saw that such a policy is often effective for developing economies. It is an anathema to market fundamentalists. Yet however much industrial policy is criticized, that approach thrives in the United States in the form of tax preferences. Corporate income taxes in the 1950s accounted for as much revenue as personal income taxes. Now that proportion is barely one-tenth of total revenue. Yet the nominal tax rate itself is relatively high by international standards. The effective rate after tax-preference subsidies, when compared to other nations, is among the lowest. Combined with lax regulation and easy formation of business, the U.S. is rated on a par with Singapore and Hong Kong in terms of being friendly for business. Likewise, personal income taxes are rife with distorting preferences — the loophole"" of mortgage interest deduction, for

---

[6] Prior to the Great Financial Crisis, there was a code in the financial sector for some of the most well-compensated risk-takers: "IBG, YBG." "I'll be gone. You'll be gone."

example. On its face it seems to benefit all the same. A moment's examination reveals, however, that the value of the benefit gets larger with the wealth and income of the taxpayer. The higher the income of the taxpayer, the greater is the marginal tax forgiveness. Luxuries such as second homes and vacation residences are included, and the amount of forgiveness itself is larger for larger homes. Prices in the marketplace do not reflect reality when they are subsidized in this manner.

Make markets visible to the private sector.

As we discussed in the previous chapter, markets do not produce public goods efficiently, not because private business cannot produce those goods, but because the nature of the goods means they escape private incentives. (Of course, roads, public facilities, military equipment and contracted services are all provided to the public sector by corporations and small businesses every day. There is a market, but it is not the competitive free market. It is an auction market.)

Likewise, basic research and development has been the stalk from which enormous technological innovation and profit — from aerospace to the Internet to biotech and nanotechnology — have flowered. The overwhelming bulk of this research was not undertaken independently by the corporations who profited, but either for the accounts of public institutions such as the U.S. Defense Department or directly by public research universities. The cost of the R&D could be assessed as an overhead charge to business activity. This is a political decision. Left alone, the current interests of already extant and dominant private actors trump the future interests of the society at large. Already extant technology is preferred over new technology. Corporations excel not at developing new technologies, but in commercializing existing ones.

Advance commitment procurement.

One way for the market to be made visible for new technologies and products is advance commitment procurement. Public agencies are large consumers of private goods. Those who need a particular product, say a bus or locomotive or a prison mattress, can request proposals to exacting specifications, such as asking for a non-polluting bus or a waste-free prison mattress. If the desired product is not forthcoming, the product is not purchased, and no expense is incurred. If it is developed and delivered, the public sector agency has what it wants and the private contractor has developed the desired technology. The same outcome can be fostered by regulation. A state can restrict the products that can be sold in its jurisdiction to those which meet environmental standards, for example. If the state is large, the motivation in the private sector to have access to that market is motivation to produce the desired technology or product.

These examples may seem fanciful, but they are not. The tremendous reduction in tailpipe emissions and the actual invention of the catalytic converter came about from California's mandate on pollution. No-waste prison mattresses were actually produced, at a cost savings after disposal was taken into consideration, through a British pilot program that simply made the specifications clear. In both cases, the public sector did no research and incurred no cost of development. In both cases, the initial reaction was, *"It is not possible, and if it were, it would be too expensive to do what you ask."* But in both cases, once the market was made visible to the private sector — a commitment to procure if the product met specifications — the product was delivered, profits were made, and society benefitted.

An Alternative Path to Development

Environmental imperative could meet global poverty reduction with a program of emerging nations building their economies using green energy and small footprint development. If new economies follow the old dirty energy path being blazed by China, they will become part of the desperate global end game. These nations could be assisted and rewarded for serving as the laboratories of sustainable development.

Firstly, a supply side Washington Consensus bias needs to be abandoned or there will be no escape from its disastrous consequences. Presently, in what some see as a cruel hoax, the developing world has been coerced into export-based, privatized economies. The success rate for such a model is remarkably thin. The historical fact is that all successful economies — from Great Britain and the U.S. to Japan and China — have employed a development model much unlike the Washington Consensus. Now we see that when the U.S. and advanced economies come face to face with the same type of economic crisis even late in their own development, they do not follow the advice they so freely gave to others. They abandon the prescription of balanced budgets and strict privatization. Necessarily the credibility of the Western sponsors of the Washington Consensus has been destroyed in much of the Third World. Investment that creates the foundations — in roads and schools and clean water — will build economies there as well as here. Other investment — in factories and plantations — is nearly always a mask for exploitation. Given an adequate platform, nations can devise their own economic success.

Forgive the debt of the Third World.
This essential first step to growth and development for many of the world's poorest nations should be executed without the restrictive structural

adjustment policies the IMF coerces. These SAPs only shackle societies to unworkable economic designs. A stable representative government that has legitimacy with its people ought to be the only criterion for debt forgiveness. Developing nations taken together now spend $13 on debt repayment for every $1 they receive in grants. This debt is often a legacy of oppressive governments or corrupt lending practices. Ending it will create immediate demand for products and a means for them to begin. Continuing the debt will continue an injustice that eats at the roots of global prosperity.

Reform trade to protect agrarian economies.

Globalization has unfortunately meant decimation of the agrarian economies of many Latin American and African countries. Agriculture is the dominant industry of most poor nations. Trade agreements must recognize this and protect agricultural development and diversification. In fact, they most go further, and encourage agriculture that is not resource- or capital-intensive and so is in line with the needs of the future. The UN's Food and Agriculture Organization has explicitly said that the leading cause of misery in the world is hunger and that the great majority of nations can feed their own people under the right trade and policy regimes. (da Silva, 2011)

Unfortunately, Globalization has meant simply a new colonialism, in which protection and subsidies are allowed for the wealthy and eliminated for the poor. The advanced countries could be exporting education, utilities, roads and machinery, rather than eviscerating the earning power of near-subsistence farmers. Immigration experience demonstrates that, in a very real sense, we will export the means of development and import products, or we will import the people.

■ ■ ■

It is a cruel myth that economic activity is orchestrated by natural laws to which governmental policy always amounts to interference, a reduction in efficiency, a distortion. Economic affairs have evolved to favor the powerful in every society. When the people are powerful, as in a free democracy, they are favored and the economy does well. When not, financial rewards cant to the dominant institution or group, and economies sputter or stall as social tensions rise.

It is, then, not populations that must bow to the natural laws of an economic galaxy. Instead the institutions, rules and incentives of the economic galaxy must be ordered to benefit populations. In our real and present case, this may allow the pursuits needed for survival and productive adaptation.

The composition of demand determines the composition of supply. A market economy would not work without freedom of demand, and it is not argued here that consumer choice should be micromanaged by government. It is argued, however, that demand ought to be influenced by the long-and short-term interests of the society and its citizens at least as much as by the pecuniary interests of large corporations. It is also argued that a free market is better understood as one with fair and open terms of use, not one dominated by those who most benefit from control.

This chapter was perhaps too short, but it is essential to understand that the market is not the remedy for a market-driven calamity. The functions of the market and its dynamism can be retained, but the economy needs to evolve in order to survive. The economy is the central organizing structure of the society. If left to the mercy of private incentives, the economy will not work for the survival of that society. We look at the shadows of the future in the next chapter.

Chapter 15:

Conclusion and Forecast

In economics, the majority is always wrong.... The only function of economic forecasting is to make astrology look respectable.

John Kenneth Galbraith

This book has been a long time coming, but it may still have arrived too soon. As it is being completed, in the early months of 2012, the economic debate is mired in confusion. The remedies applied by the monetary authorities with such conviction at the height of this crisis have proven far more expensive than effective. Fiscal policy has been diverted into a self-defeating madness of austerity. Short-term stability has been bought at the expense of long-term stagnation. Problems have not been fixed and solutions not embarked upon.

Ours has been a description of Demand Side economics as originated and developed by some of the best minds of a century, people focused on the public purpose, not distracted by personal gain. This has been a bare outline of the thinking of people who described what they saw, who responded not to their own professional prospects, but to the discipline of reason, and who followed the implications where they led.

The analysis was developed in full view of reality, and it has been proven in the cauldron of economic events. We might have included more in the way of example, but our objective was to display the history, the economists and their thought in an easily accessible way. The evidence left on the cutting room floor is compelling, and we will turn to that in our next endeavor.

There is something fundamentally disconnected, out of touch, irrelevant about an economics: that does not see demand as the inspiration of supply; that makes money cheap for a financial sector, but dear for the hungry or sick; that believes those who would borrow and those who would lend have the same interests; that views all economic activity as of the same functional value, education as good as imprisonment, health care as good as alcoholism; that thinks blood can be drawn from a stone, or nations can shrink their way to the growth; that responds to the manifest failure of its policies by calling for more of the same; that ignores those who predicted actual outcomes; and that ultimately protects the powerful and punishes the targets of their schemes. This kind of disconnected economics has its relevance and application only by the position of privilege in which it sits.

Full employment of labor is the primary indicator of a healthy economy. Fully employed labor creates its own security and minimizes the corruption and distortions, both in industry and in government. If jobs are available for all at a decent rate, there is no need for unemployment insurance, food stamps, special services for the poor who are capable of work, and so on. The public sector is completely capable of organizing the economy in a way that returns full employment to the society without depriving the private sector of impetus for innovation and growth. Indeed, full effective demand — targeted, not chaotic or captured demand — is essential for a healthy real private economy. This is prevented only by the interests of the corporate oligarchy and a financial sector which has seized effective control of public policy.

Economics is in its Dark Ages as a science. The principles of Demand Side originated with John Maynard Keynes and the pragmatists of the New Deal and were ratified by the subsequent fifty years. Those principles were corrupted and co-opted by the Neoclassical school. Like the Ptolemaic astronomers of the Medieval period, the Neoclassical school and market fundamentalists have resisted the conclusions of logic and the evidence of history. They have taught to a generation an economics that does not work. Not unlike the elaborate expansion of concentric spheres which Ptolemaic astronomers invented to keep the Earth in the center of the cosmos, an elaborate mathematics has grown up to keep the market elites at the center of the economy. Demand is at the center of the economy. Companies do not create jobs, the demand for their products creates the need to hire. Money and finance and markets need to be organized around this principle, not left to the vagaries of market appetites as manipulated for private gain.

Corporate profitability is sitting at record highs, yet hiring is anemic. Banks are fat with cash, but are not lending. Investment is tepid. Zero percent interest rates mean pensions and retirement funds are bleeding away. The debate over austerity was decided half a century ago, and it is no credit to economics as a profession that it has come again, and sadly, in virtually the same form as in the

1930s. As Steve Keen has said, *"If economics were a real science, it would have long ago been overthrown and replaced by something more realistic."* (Keen, 2011)

Here we have attempted to bring economics back into its proper context as a historical science. The outcomes of its experiments are historical outcomes. Its dynamics determine historical processes. The intellectual conceit that an invisible economic machine exists separate from the well-being of the average person is dangerous. To maintain this conceit, economists must ignore or deny what is happening. The economy is not a thermodynamic system which can be tuned by monetary policy to come to a steady state that is beneficial to all. A market-driven machine is unstable, and its fruit is not well-being, but crisis. The economy must be managed by managing demand. Raising aggregate demand to the level that eliminates unemployment and employs the capacity of the society to its full potential is the job of government and economic policy. There are no constraints, budgetary or financial or economic that prevent its happening. If World War II proved nothing more, it proved this. The debt of the U.S. rose to 120 percent of GDP. America "bailed out" the world. The experience was followed by an unprecedented growth and economic stability. Except for a brief episode in the transition period from war to peace, even inflation was subdued.

The austerity demanded of national governments today in the name of prudence or responsibility is no more prudent or responsible than eating the seed corn or allowing the barn to run to ruin. The responsible path is full employment of capacity. A fully occupied economy will best serve its citizens and is the one most capable of effectively discharging its debt. The primacy of demand is the organizing principle of Demand Side economics. Aggregate demand is by definition the sum of demand from all quarters — government, household, business — and from incomes and the net change in debt What is demanded determines what is supplied.

FORECAST

Long Term

We are bouncing along the bottom with downside risks. There is a floor under demand provided by the New Deal institutions, notably social security and unemployment insurance, and the ballast of big government, but there is no reason under current policy for economies to actually improve. That is, the bottom is sloped downward. Even presuming a turn in public policy toward reconstruction of demand, there is no robust positive path available until the great squeeze of debt is addressed and dealt with. Dealing with the debt in place will require a fundamentally different financial architecture. Replacing this current banking structure will be resisted mightily by the currently privileged financial sector, probably into a period of serious social difficulty. The financial sector and creditor nations are counting on the repayment of debt on terms that cannot be met. Since the very existence of the banks in their current form is not a feature of a reality-based economic scheme, there is no compromise which leaves them intact, and they have every incentive to press their interests as long and hard as possible. This produces a wide range of possible scenarios, most of which are in the range from very serious to catastrophic. Which is chosen depends on the political strengths. This is, as John Kenneth Galbraith has said, the defining contest between the corporation and the citizen for control of the state. Since that contest is not explicit in common understanding, its dimensions are not known. The contest may also be delayed or partially aborted if the corporations of the real economy — seeing profit, or even existence, is threatened by the debt squeeze — allow a restructuring of the financial sector and debt. That is unlikely.

There will no doubt be different dominant parties in different nations, and how this will affect the expression of the underlying conflict cannot be known. That is, a broad dissatisfaction with the orthodox solutions may result in a broad popular movement of conflict between classes, or it may be expressed in confrontations between states, or it may be expressed in irrational political movements, such as was seen in the rise of fascism in the previous Depression.

Against this, and perhaps its most significant context, is the phenomenon of global climate change. The inevitable, increasingly serious, and ultimately panic-inducing progression of climate change across the globe will cast the economic actors into different roles. The corporate oligarchy of the real sector is wedded to cheap energy and dirty technology. Its control of public policy and popular opinion cannot be overestimated. Here again, the underlying contradictions may find expression in broad social disruption, conflict between states, or irrational and violent events.

Contraction of demand from advanced economies will meet at various points the manifestations of climate change. The character of that experience will depend on an individual society's industrial and trade profile. Nations which are food importers will be exposed to disruptions in supply, whether from climate stresses or market manipulation, and a steady rise in food costs. Export-based economies, whether producers of manufactures or commodities, will find their markets shrinking. Actors within economies will face parallel reductions in earning capacity and consumption patterns.

We have not mentioned the aging of populations of advanced industrial economies around the world. This is in part a natural process of slowing population growth. It places a strain on the productive capacity for basic human needs — food, clothing, shelter, health care — at the confluence of the forces of climate change and the debt squeeze. People dependent on the current institutions and structures for their security in old age will be natural allies of the entrenched interests, even as modifications and rationalization of those institutions are needed to make the economy sound. An example might be health care in the U.S., where holders of stocks in pharmaceutical or insurance companies will be hurt when (and if) the sector is streamlined. The holders of bank stocks will be expected to resist the rationalization of that industry.

Medium Term

The only way out is the Demand Side prescription. Until that door is opened, no escape is possible. Since that door is likely to be barred for the fore-seeable future, the stagnation — bouncing along a bottom, but a bottom sloped downward which is riven with potential further crises — continues. Social unrest as the product of injustice and bad practice will grow.

In the medium term, three- to ten-year horizon, the same forces are at work: contraction of demand from falling incomes and shrinking productive debt, sectors and institutions clinging to economic and political power by whatever means possible, and the backdrop of climate-induced shortages.

In the U.S. and Europe, this means a growing realization that things will not be getting better without a change of policy, set against the regime of austerity and rigidification of current structures. That is, for example, in the U.S., the monetary authorities have favored the banking sector, made capital cheap for corporations and made every effort to expand credit (debt). The policy is a manifest failure, as incomes (including investment incomes) fall that are needed to justify the and service the debt. But even as an embarrassment of bad assets sits on its own balance sheet, the Fed under Bernanke will not change course. Although the policy is a failure, the explanation has been accepted. Thomas Palley identifies the "Neoliberal Two-Step," And it is what we have seen. The policy has failed, so what is needed is a doubling down on the policy, perhaps accompanied by the blaming of others.

The Demand Side remedies of debt write-downs, direct hiring and investment in productive public goods, including physical and social infrastructure have no natural consistency in a political process catered to the large campaign donor. Fiscal policy has thus been predominantly slanted to aid the corporate sector, by means of tax cuts and bailouts of major players along with support to consumer demand via payroll and personal income tax reductions. Consequently, fiscal policy has been ineffective in stimulating a recovery. Being ineffective, all fiscal policy options are further from prospect than they were at the outset of the Obama presidency in 2009.

In Europe, the austerities imposed as conditions for loans and cures for the banking crisis and the debt and trade imbalances instead produced recession. Falling incomes and reduced demand have made matters worse. There again the orchestra of the ECB and the creditor countries has struck up the Neoliberal Two Step. Austerity made matters worse, so the answer is to extend austerity. The outcome is likely to be a stronger banking presence, rather than a restructuring of banks, and a shift of private debts onto public balance sheets. The "reforms" of lower wages and smaller pensions will be chosen over debt restructuring and controls on capital flows.

In the developing world, again, climate stress and adverse conditions of trade will create tragic scenarios for countries across the globe. Export markets will weaken for the newly industrialized and the commodity producers, ending a short period of relative well-being. Those dependent on food imports will suffer most. This means serious instability in places like China and the Middle East. The exception may be Latin American, led by Brazil, whose principle difficulty in the medium term may be dealing with eager capital inflows from the rest of the world looking for returns from the only healthy region remaining.

Short Term

Many have suggested we are in danger of repeating the mistakes of 1937, which anticipated the end of the Great Depression with austerity policies that generated another leg down. Clearly, from the Demand Side, we are still not past 1933. We are in the period prior to coming to grips with the full scale of the problem. We are nearer the beginning than the end.

Employment will track the change in credit, as it has over the past thirty years, and as we learned from Steve Keen. Incomes are stagnant or falling for the great majority, so the change in credit will be the change in demand. In this regard, we have seen the U.S. benefit from the problems of Europe and in the developing economies, as capital flees to the "safe haven" of the dollar. GDP will likewise reflect the change in credit. As we've seen, however, GDP does not appropriately measure experience, and the underlying condition of the economy is sharply negative, as resources (including the air, water, soil and natural systems of the Commons) are being drained, even as public goods and market structures are deteriorating.

Monetary policy seeks to inflate debt ("produce credit") and increase risk. This leads to an inflation of liquid asset prices which inflates the wealth of those with assets and increases the disparity between rich and poor. This increasing inequality is itself inefficient, as we saw, and reinforces the downturn. The monetary authorities in the U.S. are preoccupied with these markets, and each new indication of weakness is met with more easy money. The economy has struck a reef and is sinking. The herd of the market is rushing from one side of the boat to the other. The captains at the Fed are seeking to calm this herd. They are not preparing lifeboats, even changing course, or cutting engine speed, let alone setting about a repair to the hull. Unfortunately, the herd on deck are the first class passengers, and those below are facing truly desperate times.

At present, while robust markets for stocks, bonds, and increasingly commodities may be seen as indicators of economic well-being by some, they are in fact floating on official injections of ever-increasing amounts of liquidity. Cheaper credit and central bank purchases of financial instruments must have a limit. When that limit is reached, financial assets must fall. When they do, it is inevitable that the public sector, the taxpayer, will find huge private liabilities have once again become their responsibility.

The government's fiscal policy, which should be the avenue of recovery, is stalled in consumer and corporate-centric schemes. For all their ineffectiveness, the end of these, now scheduled for the end of 2012, is being characterized as a "fiscal cliff," even by orthodox economists, that will reduce GDP by two to five percent. In an epic play of cart before the horse, governments which socialized the damage done by private financial houses during the Great Financial Crisis are apparently going to be the scapegoats for the continuing crisis.

In Europe, where banks are extremely unstable and the willingness to address the underlying issues is confounded by a misunderstanding of those issues, it is hard to know how soon the issues will come to a point. We follow Nouriel Roubini in suggesting restructuring for Portugal, Ireland, Spain, Italy and perhaps others exposed to imbalances will shake the *euro*, and perhaps destroy that currency or chase it into Northern Europe.

Overview

Stagnating and falling incomes, increasing debt loads, deteriorating public goods, depletion of the Commons, the influences are the same, whether short-, medium-, or long-term. The differences lie in the relative political power of the various interest groups. But here also there must be an inflection point. And we may be closer than we think.

Markets, particularly financial markets, have been captured by the biggest players. Those players have captured government itself, its regulators and legislatures, so the bias to private investment continues. But the high returns to investments are in public goods; the capacity to produce private goods is overbuilt.[1]

Again, the global economy is bouncing along a bottom, but a bottom that is itself sloped downward. The debt that burdens private households and governments acts as a vacuum pulling the economy down, with the assurance of crisis after crisis until and unless we adopt the Demand Side prescription. An enormous Ponzi debt, founded on rising asset prices, not on real returns, makes the financial sector across the world insolvent in large part. Attempts by the lenders to collect on debt that cannot be paid can only fail. The more fervently they are pursued, the worse the near-term contraction, and the more desperate the social environment.

The banking sector currently controls much of public policy across the globe. As the banking crisis becomes more apparent, however, and the contest becomes more defined, we will be able to see more clearly which way we are headed.

■ ■ ■

If we are wrong, some combination of monetary policy and market power will revive the economies of the world in the coming years. The central banks' absorption of private losses will not blow up in the public's face. The "Market" of financial interests will somehow find reason and ability to expand credit while at the same time extracting payment on bad debts through austerity. The world will divide into an extremely privileged upper class and an increasingly deprived lower class without social unrest. It will be hard, but ultimately the unemployment, sacrifice and suffering will lead us into the light.

If we are right, economies will career ever more unstably along a downward path until a decision point. Two possibilities then present themselves. Both come with wholesale destruction of financial wealth. The Ponzi value of assets cannot be sustained.

In the first possibility, the primacy of demand and the imperative to full

---

[1] Thomas Palley has identified a demand gap which demonstrates that the shortfall in demand from reliance on the supply side has been filled by ever-greater private investment, sponsored by ever-lower interest rates, and ever more accommodative taxation and regulation. Rates have become zero and yet there is no private investment in prospect to fill that gap. (Palley T. I., 2012)

employment are realized in action. This may come about, as in the Depression, by simple compassion combined with political necessity, or it may be lit by economic understanding. With this possibility, the debt is dealt with directly. Full and appropriate employment becomes the driver, not a frightened passenger. Financial losses in this case may be structured and mitigated by a general tax, perhaps the tax of inflation.

In the second possibility, the demand for change is diverted by some of the current entrenched interests through scapegoating others. This results in a disorganized, chaotic period. The outcomes in this scenario are impossible to predict.

When John Maynard Keynes wrote in the 1930s, the challenge was poverty and want set side-by-side with a market-driven idleness. Keynes advocated expanding demand through the public sector. This approach was ultimately ratified by the Second World War, the largest public works project in history. Subsequent to the war, the Demand Side prescription was followed, then diluted, gradually co-opted and eventually discarded. The management of demand was turned over to an expansion of private investment with its bias toward the investing class. In the latter part of this period came the financialization of the economy identified by Soros, Galbraith and others here, characterized by Ponzi finance (Minsky's term for debt incurred in the expectation of price rises), not hedge finance (his term for debt incurred for productive purposes). By no coincidence, at the same time has arrived an extreme financial instability, high unemployment and unprecedented disparities in incomes. The middle class of the early post-war period is no longer with us.

But now we have the additional challenge of climate change. A degradation of the natural systems upon which the human race depends looms before us. Keynes did not anticipate climate change. (Keynes also imagined a world without war and one with a stable population.) But this is a calamity potentially even greater than that met by the Second World War. Climate dislocations may, in fact, be played out in wars and social conflict, but will be experienced also in widespread and savage hunger and thirst and disease, in planetary migration, unknowable weather, and almost unthinkable collapses of natural systems. In the best of worlds, this will be a challenge the equivalent of World War II, a public works project that will again ratify Demand Side economics. In the worst, the dead religion of the free market will continue to be used to justify the corporate oligarchy and a continued run to ruin.

Consumer capitalism, where a corporate oligarchy dominates and private goods are the sole virtue, is dead at its own hand. Demand Side economics, just as it did in World War II, can organize the society to the new reality, with the promise of peace and prosperity beyond.

Afterword

Demand Side Exposed —
The Confessions of an Unreconstructed Progressive Economist

I wanted to study economics from early in my academic career, but even as an undergraduate I could see that the discipline of economics, as taught at least at the large state university I attended, was ill-suited to the real world. An episode in which the only radical economist on the faculty was purged, a man whose classes were full of engaged students, darkened the experience. The economics major seemed to be a discipline for people to learn things that other people could not understand, so to achieve job security. In four years in the early 1990s I heard the name Keynes mentioned only twice in lecture, and then it was mispronounced. (It's KANES, not KEENS.)

Suspecting they might be hiding the good and useful stuff, I persevered. The cabinets with the curriculum connected to the real world remained locked, and I never got the keys. Later I was to discover the cabinets were empty. The assumptions that could not stand up to the common sense of a college freshman underlay the entire field. Critical gaps in reasoning were puttied in with wishful thinking or outright error. The theoretical fabric of economics as a science was woven with these feeble threads. At the same time I came up against a personal reality. I was already in my forties with family.

I looked out at the elementary assumptions of perfectly competitive markets and perfect information and saw how it plainly did not correspond to even one real world situation. Monopoly and oligopoly ruled. Even restaurants were rewarded more for location and less for quality of food or service. Prices in the real world responded less to supply and demand and more to manipulation by market power or government regulation and subsidy — or to macro forces outside the individual markets.

Economics I could see even then was a science of human behavior. Mathematics was suitable for thermodynamics or Newtonian physics, but plainly in a system that was not closed and where there were no independent variables unless by assumption, the math's application to economics worked only in a hypothetical world. And for all the precision of the econometric models and their complete fit to the statistics of the past, the results were miserable when applied to the future. (I was to discover that this failure of mathematics could be mitigated by introducing real world mimics of dynamics and historic time vs. the ignoring of time, or at best using chronological T, T+1, T+2... time.) My later forecasting dictum was borrowed from Keynes. "*Better to be approximately right than precisely wrong.*" Precisely wrong is what most economics and economic fore-casting is today. On the other hand, when I hear today's complaint that forecasting cannot be very accurate and suffers from some intrinsic and unknowable randomness, I remember the sobriquet of Karl Popper (by way of George Soros): "*Forecasts and explanations are symmetrical and reversible.*" I take this to mean if your forecasts are no good, then your explanations are no good.

The economic lions of the profession at the time I studied were at the University of Chicago — followers of Milton Friedman and Robert Lucas and others; Monetarism, Rational Expectations, Efficient Market Theory, and so on. This book was not organized as a debate with these schools, but they are in-escapable adversaries on the way to clear economic thinking, and others have taken on that job. The Neoclassical school is dominant, but there is a vigorous and insightful minority pointing out the error. Some of those we featured here: John Maynard Keynes, Leon Keyserling, John Kenneth Galbraith, Hyman Minsky, Joseph Stiglitz, James K. Galbraith, George Soros, Steve Keen and Nouriel Roubini. There are others as well, though not as long a list as one would like. Joan Robinson, James Tobin, Thomas Palley, Robert Kuttner, Robert Pollin, Michael Hudson, Paul Davidson, and more.

Perhaps it was my experience in the real world, where I had a list of jobs from cabs, to restaurants, to mines, to forestry, to municipal government that made me aware that these theories did not flower in the places people made their livings, but only in the hothouses of Wall Street and sponsored endowments. It is my firm belief that many if not most students found academic economics equally invalid, or at a minimum, dreadfully uninteresting. Certainly the business school and the economics department did not cross-pollinate.

I did well in the undergraduate curriculum by granting it the benefit of the doubt. I was convinced that once through the fundamentals and when the weak in spirit were weeded out, the elect would emerge into a realm where the absurd assumptions were revisited and the tools became applicable. Never happened.

My particular school did not have a parallel graduate curriculum for heretics or even for those interested in the real world. It was to be mathematics and theory or nothing. There were no other schools in our region offering PhD's. It would be math and facile theory or nothing.

The choice I made was to take my high grades and new degree to work with me on the bus, and to study the alternatives outside Academia. I found (and did not invent) the lineage of economic thought, which I refer to as Demand Side economics, that has progressed and become more useful over time.

The current crisis is doubly frustrating. It confirms my assessment of the state of economic science, but it is disheartening to witness the absence of widespread revision of the thinking that got us here. The discipline of economics is forever stained by Monetarism and the market-driven ideology that devised the charts and hired the captains in the Fed and elsewhere that have brought the ship of the economy onto the rocks. Indeed, the decline of U.S. industry and the stagnation of median incomes, the decline of social infrastructure and the rise of a parasitic financial sector has been considered a golden period, the "Great Moderation," by most economists.

Those who identified the weaknesses and predicted the breakdown get to say, "*I told you so*," but the orthodox mainstream hears only what it wants to hear. High Academia and the halls of Wall Street seem to be the repository for self-serving ignorance, not for workable economics. We continue to look to the same failed conceptual framework for answers.

On one hand, it is logical to be discouraged and frustrated. On the other hand, we see around us the rubble of an intellectual conceit. On the highest points still standing sit the architects who built the structure and claimed it would last forever. There ought to be no confusion as to responsibility. At least intellectually. But economics is a full-contact sport, not a theoretical nicety. As we've seen, it is dominated by entrenched interests and motivations quite other than the search for efficiency and fairness. But the opportunity is there. John Kenneth Galbraith once said, "*Every successful revolution is the kicking in of a rotten door.*" This door is certainly rotten. Who will do the kicking and what the result will be is still to be determined.

In this book I hope to have offered the views of those not favored by academic elites or corporate subsidies. I hope to have consolidated the views of those who make sense, displayed the evidence that proves them right, and done it in a way that is accessible and useful to the reader's own understanding. It is not simply that we must escape the errors of the past, no matter how great. We must also move aggressively into a productive and sustainable future.

END

Bibliography

Bernanke, B. (2000). *Essays on the Great Depression.* Princeton, NJ: Princeton University Press.

Bernanke, B. (2010). On the Implications of the Financial Crisis for Economics. *Conference co-sponsored by the Center for Economic Policy Studies and the Bendheim Center for Finance.* Princeton, NJ: U.S. Federal Reserve.

Blanchard, O., Dell'Ariccia, & Mauro. (2010). Rethinking Macroeconomic Policy. *Journal of Money Credit and Banking* , 207.

Blinder, A., & Zandi, M. (2010). *How the Great Recession Was Brought to an End.* July 27, 2010, p.16.

Bloomberg. (2009, January 30). Roubini Sees Global Gloom After Davos Vindication. *Bloomberg, Simon Kennedy* .

Brokaw, T. (1998). *The Greatest Generation.* New York: Random House.

da Silva, J. G. (1924, July 24). Interview. *Business Daily, BBC* .

Economist. (2010, March 18). *The Economist* .

Eurostat. (2012). *Eurostat http://epp.eurostat.ec.europa.eu/cache/ITY_PUBLIC/2-26042011-AP/EN/2-26042011-AP-EN.PDF,accessed February 28, 2012.* Eurostat.

Federal Reserve. (n.d.). http://www.federalreserve.gov/faqs/about_14986.htm.

Financial Crisis Inquiry Commission. (2011). *"Conclusions of the Financial Crisis Inquiry Commission," in The Final Report of the National Commission on the Causes of the Financial and Economic Crisis in the United States.* Washington, D.C.: Official Government Edition.

Fisher, I. (1933). The Debt-Deflation Theory of Great Depressions. *Econometrica* , 1(4), 337-57.].

Galbraith, J. K. (1973). *Economics and the Public Purpose.* Boston: Houghton Mifflin Company.

Galbraith, J. K. (1987). *Economics In Perspective: A Critical History.* Boston: Houghton Mifflin Company.

Galbraith, J. K. (2008). Interview. *Bill Moyers Journal, October 24, 2008* .

Galbraith, J. K. (2010). Remarks. *Bernard Schwarz Symposium, October 20, 2010* .

Galbraith, J. K. (1967). *The New Industrial State.* Boston: Houghton Mifflin Company.

Galbraith, J. K. (2008). *The Predator State.* Free Press.

Greenspan, A. (2010). Remarks in a discussion with Gerald Corrigan and Ben Bernanke, November 6, 2010. *A Return to Jekyll Island.* webcast: http://www.frbatlanta.org/news/co: Federal Reserve Bank of Atlanta and Rutgers University.

Greenspan, A. (2010). The Crisis. *The Brookings Institution* .

Holmes, A. (1969). Operational Constraints on the Stabilization of Money Supply Growth.

Controlling Monetary Aggregates, Nantucket Island: The federal Reserve Bank of Boston , 65-77.

Ireland, P. (2011). A New Keynesian Perspective on the Great Recession. *Journal of Money, Credit and Banking* , 43(1): 41-54.

Johnson, S., & Kwak, J. (2010). *13 Bankers.* New York: Pantheon Books.

Keen, S. (2001). *Debunking Economics: The Naked Emperor of the Social Sciences.* Australia: Pluto Press.

Keen, S. (2011). Dude, Where is My Recovery. *Debtwatch, June 11, 2011* .

Keen, S. (2001). Economists Have No Ears. *Post-Autistic Economics Newsletter* , Issue No. 7.

Keen, S. (2011, October 1). One Million Economists Can Be Wrong: The Free Trade Fallacy. *Real World Economics Review* .

Keynes, J. M. (1920). *The Economic Consequences of the Peace.* New York: Harcourt, Brace and Howe.

Keynes, J. M. (1936). *The General Theory of Employment, Interest and Money.* London: MacMillan and Company Limited.

Keyserling, L. H. (1975). *Full Employment Without Inflation.* Washington, D.C.: Conference on Economic Progress.

Keyserling, L. H. (1971). *Leon H. Keyserling Oral History Interviews -- Conducted by Jerry N. Hess.* Truman Library.

Keyserling, L. H. (1980). *Money, Credit and Interest Rates: Their Gross Mismanagement by the Federal Reserve System.* Washington, D.C.: Conference on Economic Progress.

Kochar, R. R. (2011). *Wealth Gaps Rise to Record Highs Between Whites, Blacks, Hispanics.* Pew Research Center.

Koo, R. C. (2011). [FN: For a description of the flows of debt and borrowing, see Richard C. Koo, "The world in balance sheet recession: causes, cure, and politics. *Real World Economics Review* , December 2011, p. 19.

Krugman, P., & Eggertsson, G. B. (n.d.). Debt, Deleveraging, and the Liquidity Trap: A Fisher-Minsky-Koo Approach. *Draft* .

McKibbin, W. a. (2009). Modelling the Global Financial Crisis. *Oxford Review of Economic Policy* , 25(4): 581-607.

Minsky, H. P. (1982). *Can "It" Happen Again?: Essays on instability anf finance.* Armonk: M.E. Sharpe.

Minsky, H. P. (1975). *John Maynard Keynes.* New York: Columbia University Press.

Minsky, H. P. (1986). *Stabilizing an Unstable Economy.* Cambridge, MA: Yale University Press.

Oswald, A., Caruth, A., & Hooker, M. (1998). Input Prices and Unemployment Equilibria: Theory and Evidence for the United States. *Review of Economics and Statistics* , 80, 621-628.

Palley, T. I. (2012). *From Financial Crisis to Stagnation.* London: Cambridge University Press.

Palley, T. (2010). Remarks. *Bernard Schwartz Symposium, October, 2010.)* .

Ramonet, I. (1998, November). The Politics of Hunger. *Le Monddiplomatique* .

Rodrik, D. (2002). *Feasible Globalizations.* Cambridge: Harvard University.

Rodrik, D. (2007). *One Economics, Many Recipes: Globalization Institutions and Economic Growth.* Princeton, NJ: Princeton University Press.

Rogoff, K., & Reinhardt, C. (2009). *This Time is Different: Eight Centuries of Financial Folly.* Princeton, NJ: Princeton University Press.

Roubini, N. a. (2004). *Bailouts or Bail-Ins: Responding to Financial Crises in Emerging Economies.* Peterson Institute.

Roubini, N. (2011, November 11). Down with the Eurozone. *Project Syndicate* .

Roubini, N. (2008, January 23). Goldilocks and the Three Ugly Bears; A Year Later at Davos. *Wall Street Journal* .

Roubini, N. (2006). Presentation. *World Economic Forum, January 27, 2006.* Davos, Switzerland.

Roubini, N., & Mihm, S. (2010). *Crisis Economics: A Crash Course in the Future of Finance.* New York: Penguin.

Roubini, N., & Setser, B. W. (2004). *Bailouts or Bail-Ins: Responding to Financial Crises in Emerging Economies.* Peterson Institute.

Roubini, N., Alpert, D. A., & Hockett, R. (2011, October). The Way Forward: Moving from the Post-Bubble, Post-Bust Economy to Renewed Growth and Competitiveness. *New America Foundation* .

Sarkozy Commission. (2009). *Final Report of the Commission on the Measurement of Economic Performance and Social Progress.* http://stiglitz-sen-fitoussi.fr/documents/rapport_anglais.pdf.

Say, J. B. (1803). *A Treatise on Political Economy.*

Schor, J. (2011). Economics for the 99%. *Occupy Harvard, December 12, 2011.* Cambridge, MA.

Schumpeter, J. (1942). *Capitalism, Socialism and Democracy.* London: Routledge.

Schumpeter, J. (1934). *The Theory of Economic Development: An inquiry into profits, capital, credit, interest and the business cycle.* Cambridge, MA: Harvard University Press.

Skidelsky, R. (2009). *Interview with Tom Keene.* Bloomberg on the Economy.

Soros, G. (2009). *Lecture October 27, 2009.* Central European University.

Soros, G. (1998). *The Crisis of Global Capitalism: Open Society Endangered.* Public Affairs.

Soros, G. (2008). *The New Paradigm for Financial Markets: The Credit Crisis of 2008 and What*

It Means. Public Affairs.

Stiglitz, J. (2011). *"Macroeconomics in Crisis," presentation to the Central European CERGE, October 11, 2011.* Central European CERGE.

Stiglitz, J. E. (2009). *Final Report: The commission on the Measurement of Economic Performance and Social Progress.*

Stiglitz, J. E. (2010). *Freefall.* New York: W.W. Norton & Company.

Stiglitz, J. E. (2002). *Globalization and Its Discontents.* New York: W.W. Norton & Co.

Stiglitz, J. E. (2006). *Making Globalization Work.* New York: W.W. Norton & Company.

(1945). *Summary Report, United States Strategic Bombing Survey.* Washington, D.C.: U.S. Government Printing Office.

Tobin, J. (1972). A Proposal for International Monetary Reform. *Eastern Economic Journal* , 153–159.

UNICEF. (1999). *The State of the World's Children.* New York: UNICEF.

Wilkinson, R., & Pickett, K. (2009). *The Spirit Level: Why Greater Equality Makes Societies Stronger.* New York: Bloomsbury Press.

Zandi, M. a. (2010, July 27). How the Great Recession Was Brought to an End. *Report* , p. 16.

www.ingramcontent.com/pod-product-compliance
Lightning Source LLC
Chambersburg PA
CBHW051501170526
45166CB00001B/341